GORDON JARVIE began his career as an English teacher, later working as a publisher and writer. His books include the *Bloomsbury Grammar Guide* (2nd edn 2007) and other language titles; *Scottish Folk and Fairy Tales* (2nd edn 2007); and *The Scottish Reciter* (1993), which this collection replaces and updates. He has edited various other anthologies, and with his wife he has written several *Scottie Books* for children. His most recent poetry pamphlet is *The Tale of the Crail Whale* (for more information about his poetry see www.scottish-pamphlet-poetry.com). He lives in the East Neuk of Fife.

100
FAVOURITE
SCOTTISH POEMS
TO READ OUT LOUD

EDITED BY GORDON JARVIE

Luath Press Limited
EDINBURGH
www.luath.co.uk

First published 2007
Reprinted 2014
Reprinted 2015
Reprinted 2016

ISBN (10): 1-906307-01-6
ISBN (13): 978-1-906307-01-1

The publishers acknowledge the support of

 Scottish
Arts Council

towards the publication of this volume.

The paper used in this book is recyclable. It is made from low-chlorine
pulps produced in a low-emission manner from renewable forests.

Printed and bound by
Bell & Bain Ltd., Glasgow

Typeset in ITC Charter and Gill Sans by
3btype.com

To Frances,
still my own red, red rose

CONTENTS

Notes

Index of Poets

ACKNOWLEDGEMENTS

Our thanks are due to the following authors, publishers and estates who have generously given permission to reproduce poems:

James Aitchison, 'Landscape with Lapwings' from *Spheres* (Chatto & Windus, 1975), reproduced courtesy of the author; Marion Angus, 'The Fox's Skin' from *The Singin' Lass: Selected Works of Marion Angus* (Polygon, 2006), reproduced courtesy of Birlinn Ltd, www.birlinn.co.uk; J. K. Annand, 'Heron' and 'Street Talk' from *Bairn Rhymes* (Mercat Press, 1998), both reproduced courtesy of Scottish Language Dictionaries; Meg Bateman, 'Elgol: Two Views' from *Soirbheas: Fair Wind* (Polygon, 2007), reproduced courtesy of Polygon, an imprint of Birlinn Ltd, www.birlinn.co.uk; Sheena Blackhall, 'The Only Bloody Hill in Scotland' reproduced courtesy of the author; George Bruce, 'Kinnaird Head' and 'Love in Age' from *Today Tomorrow: Collected Poems* (Polygon, 2001), reproduced courtesy of Polygon, an imprint of Birlinn Ltd, www.birlinn.co.uk; George Campbell Hay, 'The Smoky Smirr o Rain' from *Collected Poems and Songs* (Edinburgh University Press, 2000), reproduced courtesy of Edinburgh University Press, www.eup.ed.ac.uk; Stewart Conn, 'Choral Symphony' from *In the Kibble Palace* (Bloodaxe, 1987), reproduced courtesy of the author; C. M. Costie, 'The Peerie Grandson' from *Orkney Dialect Tales of C. M. Costie* (Kirkwall Press, 1976), reproduced courtesy of Mrs Annie G. Scott; Robert Crawford, 'Alba Einstein' and 'Scotland' from *Selected Poems* (Jonathan Cape, 2005), both reprinted by permission of The Random House Group Ltd; Jenni Daiches, 'On Beinn an Eoin' from *Mediterranean* (Scottish Cultural Press, 1995), reproduced courtesy of the author; Kirkpatrick Dobie, 'My Father' from *Selected Poems* (Peterloo, 1992), reproduced courtesy of Peterloo; Lesley Duncan, 'Wilful Will', reproduced courtesy of the author; Matthew Fitt, 'Blethertoun Rovers' first published in *Blethertoun Braes* (Itchy Coo, 2004), reproduced by kind permission from Itchy Coo/Black & White Publishing; Douglas J. Fraser, 'Highland Landscape' from *Landscape of Delight* (Macdonald of Loanhead, 1967), reproduced courtesy of Mrs Heather Moncur; G. S. Fraser, 'Home Town Elegy: For Aberdeen in Spring' from *Poems of G. S. Fraser* (Leicester University Press, 1981), reproduced courtesy of Eileen Fraser; Duncan Glen, 'Stranger in Toun' from *Collected Poems* (Akros, 2006), reproduced courtesy of Akros; Sydney Goodsir Smith, 'Brooding Rebuked', from his *Collected Poems* (John Calder, 1975), reproduced courtesy of

Calder Publications; Margaret Green, 'The Ballad of Janitor MacKay' from *The Kist* (Learning & Teaching Scotland, 1996), reproduced courtesy of the author; Hamish Henderson, 'Ballad of the Men of Knoydart' from *Collected Poems and Songs* (Curly Snake Publishing, 2000), reproduced courtesy of Mrs Felicity Henderson; William Hershaw, 'Songs of the Scottish Exam Board English Marker' and 'Parents' Night', from *The Cowdenbeath Man* (Scottish Cultural Press, 1997), reproduced courtesy of the author; Violet Jacob, 'The Poacher to Orion' from *Voices From Their Ain Countrie* (Association for Scottish Literary Studies, 2006), reproduced courtesy of Malcolm Hutton; Gordon Jarvie, 'Walking in the Botanic Gardens, Glasgow' and 'Yesterday in Laggan' from *Room for a Rhyme from Time to Time* (Harpercroft, 2004) and 'The Angels' Share' from *The Tale of the Crail Whale* (Harpercrpft, 2006), all reproduced courtesy of the author; Jackie Kay, 'Old Tongue' from *Other Lovers* (Bloodaxe Books, 1993), reproduced courtesy of Bloodaxe Books; Stuart Kermack, 'Foreword' from *Sonnets for My Son* (Pinkfoot Press, 2001), reproduced courtesy of Pinkfoot Press; Bill Keys, 'A Dug a Dug', reproduced courtesy of Mrs May Keys; R. D. Laing, 'Sonnet' from *Sonnets* (Michael Joseph, 1979), reproduced courtesy of The R. D. Laing Estate; Tom Leonard, 'The Qualification' and 'Unrelated Incidents No. 6' from *Intimate Voices: Selected Work 1965–1983* (Galloping Dog Press, 1984), reproduced courtesy of the author; Maurice Lindsay, 'Speaking of Scotland' from *Collected Poems* (Paul Harris, 1974), reproduced courtesy of the author; Liz Lochhead, 'Poem for my sister' from *Dreaming Frankenstein and Collected Poems* (Polygon, 1994) and 'Kidspoem/Bairnsang' from *The Colour of Black and White* (Polygon, 2005), both reproduced courtesy of Polygon, an imprint of Birlinn Ltd, www.birlinn.co.uk; Norman MacCaig, 'My Last Word on Frogs' and 'July Evening' from *The Poems of Norman MacCaig* (Polygon, 2005) and 'Ballade of Good Whisky' from *Collected Poems* (Chatto & Windus, 1993), all reproduced courtesy of Polygon, an imprint of Birlinn Ltd, www.birlinn.co.uk; Carl MacDougall, 'Cod-liver Oil and Orange Juice', reproduced courtesy of the author; Ian McFadyen, 'The First Hoolit's Prayer' from *The Kist* (Learning & Teaching Scotland, 1996), reproduced courtesy of the author; Ellie McDonald, 'Uncle' from *The Gangan Fuit* (Chapman, 1991), reproduced courtesy of Chapman; Matt McGinn, 'The Wee Kirkcudbright Centipede', reproduced courtesy of Mrs Janette McGinn; Edwin Morgan, 'Strawberries' from *Collected Poems* (Carcanet, 1990), reproduced courtesy of Carcanet Press Ltd and 'Open the doors!' from *Voyage of Intent* (Luath, 2005), reproduced courtesy of Luath Press

Ltd; Edwin Muir, 'The Confirmation' from *Collected Poems* (Faber & Faber, 1960), reproduced courtesy of Faber & Faber; Stephen Mulrine, 'A Gude Buke' from *Poems* (Akros, 1971), reproduced courtesy of the author; Charles Murray, 'Bennachie' from *Hamewith: The Complete Poems of Charles Murray* (Aberdeen University Press, 1979), reproduced courtesy of the Charles Murray Memorial Fund; Nancy Nicolson, 'Listen Tae the Teacher' from *The Kist* (Learning & Teaching Scotland, 1996), reproduced courtesy of the author; Will H. Ogilvie, 'The Hill Road to Roberton' and 'On a Roman Helmet' from *The Border Poems of W. H. Ogilvie* (1922), reproduced courtesy of Catherine Reid; Don Paterson, 'Waking with Russell' from *Landing Light* (Faber & Faber, 2003), reproduced courtesy of Faber & Faber; David C. Purdie, 'The Biggers', reproduced courtesy of the author; John Purser, 'In Winter', reproduced courtesy of the author; Tessa Ransford, 'Life Summertime' from *Natural Selection* (Akros, 2001), reproduced courtesy of the author; James Robertson, 'Wee Davie Daylicht' from *Blethertoun Braes* (Itchy Coo, 2004), reproduced by kind permission from Itchy Coo/Black & White Publishing and 'The Vision of Enric Miralles' from *Voyage of Intent* (Luath, 2005), reproduced courtesy of Luath Press Ltd; Syd Scroggie, 'Ante Mortem' from *Give Me the Hills* (David Winter & Son, 1978), reproduced courtesy of Mrs Margaret Scroggie; William Soutar, 'The Gowk', reproduced courtesy of the National Library of Scotland; Raymond Vettese, 'A Pan Drop Man', reproduced courtesy of the author; Colin Will, 'The Legacy' from *Thirteen Ways of Looking at the Highlands* (Diehard, 1996), reproduced courtesy of the author.

Every effort has been made to trace the copyright holders of poems published in this book. If any material has been included without the appropriate acknowledgement, the publishers would be glad to correct this in future editions.

INTRODUCTION

Lots of lucky people imbibe and memorise poetry, and then file it away until such time as they are called on to recite it. This anthology is for poorer mortals – like myself – who are not blessed with total recall, and need a handy prop when the cry goes up: 'And now for a recitation!'

Reading aloud is still practised here and there, encouraged by Burns Nights, St Andrew's Day celebrations, Halloween, National Poetry Day events, StAnza and other poetry slams, as well as ceilidhs, singsongs and school events. But too many schools appear to have forgotten that reading aloud helps students develop public-speaking skills, build self-confidence, and learn about their literary heritage. Nowadays many classrooms need to find their way back to the appreciation of a repertoire of well spoken, well loved verses.

As well as newer or less well known texts, this collection tries to offer an agreeable element of re-discovery. So there are old ballads and narratives here, such as 'The Four Maries', 'Lord Ullin's Daughter' and 'The Bonny House o Airlie'; favourite love songs, such as 'Annie Laurie' and 'Mary of Argyll'; hymns and anthems, such as 'The 23rd Psalm'; and walking songs such as 'The Road and the Miles to Dundee'. Most of us know a few lines from these poems; here are the full texts. And interspersed with these old favourites are many more recent poems, culled from the huge range and variety that is contemporary Scottish poetry.

Whose favourites? Well, this anthology is a personal selection and makes no attempt to include all the usual suspects. That would require a much bigger project. The book is worked around the kind of public poetry that can be well conveyed to audiences that may not have a copy of the text in front of them. It includes some of the 'occasional' poetry that used to be written specifically for recitation or singing at concerts and soirées – represented here by the work of writers like Charles Murray, J. M. Caie, William Graham, Hilton Brown and Jimmy Copeland.

Many readers will recall the Norman MacCaig anecdote in which, as a young man, Norman asked an Edinburgh neighbour what he thought of his poems (he had recently presented the neighbour with an autographed copy of his first book). The neighbour pronounced the book very interesting, but added the killer question, 'When are you publishing the answers?' None of *that* kind of poetry is included here, because it tends not to work well in the context of a public reading. And of course Norman quickly moved beyond that kind of poetry, so his later work is well represented here.

This collection is an update of an earlier anthology I had the pleasure of editing, called *The Scottish Reciter* (1993). There I drew attention to the work of many poets whose work seemed notoriously hard to find in commercially produced books. It remains an aim of this selection to spotlight some of these writers, and not to let the 'canon' get too narrow; too many of us still seem unaware of the delights of poets like Ellie McDonald, Bill Hershaw, Wilma Horsbrugh, Will H. Ogilvie, Matt McGinn, Bill Keys and Stephen Mulrine, to say nothing of the 'occasional' poets listed earlier.

In *The Scottish Reciter* the poems were organised in sections: Narrative and the ballads, Lyric and song, Robert Burns, Young reciter, Glasgow poets, and 'Mixter-maxter'. The present collection is a 'mixter-maxter' from 1 to 100, following the example of Stewart Conn's impressive recent collection (*100 Favourite Scottish Poems*, 2006). None of Stewart's choice of poems is included here, although 24 of his poets are; along with 40+ poets not featured in his selection. So here I have tried deliberately to fish a slightly different part of the ocean.

It is hard to categorise poems too baldly as being 'about' something specific, but a rough breakdown of this selection may be attempted thus:

1 – 8	Statements old and new, about Scotland
9 – 16	Families – sisters, fathers, uncles, grandchildren ...
17 – 24	Love poems
25 – 36	Dogs, birds, fish, frogs, centipedes ...
37 – 45	Trains and trades
46 – 55	Schools and language

No doubt a listing like the above offers hostages to fortune. So be it. Yes, some poems could fit under different headings. And yes, 24 does sit very well with 94, and vice versa. (And so forth.) But all that is for the reader to work out. Reading aloud is about finding texts that say something to *you*, texts that you are comfortable with. In normal circumstances, especially if you're new to the game, it is best when reading aloud to choose a text that gives *you* pleasure; you are then free to concentrate on trying to communicate some of that pleasure. There is one don't: never try to read aloud a text you dislike, because you won't enjoy the experience and neither will your listeners. (Unless of course you are an Equity-registered thespian, and then you can do a send-up ...) Reading aloud is also about finding texts that suit the event or occasion at which you propose to read them. It is about introducing your text appropriately to your listeners; the notes at the back of this collection may prove helpful in this context. And try, ahead of the reading, to decide if you are going to read the text straight or for laughs, or as a tear-jerker. Practise the Scots (if necessary), the stresses, the pauses, the intonations. A few rehearsals (even if only in front of your mirror) should help you on your way.

My thanks go to Gavin MacDougall, Catriona Vernal and colleagues at Luath for their enthusiasm for this project and for steering it to publication; and to all the poets who have agreed to be included in the book. Thanks are also due to Lizzie MacGregor of the Scottish Poetry Library and Tegwen Wallace of Learning and Teaching Scotland for their help in the tracing of copyright holders. I hope readers will enjoy the collection as much as I have enjoyed putting it together.

Gordon Jarvie
October 2007

1

OPEN THE DOORS!

Edwin Morgan b.1920

Open the doors!
Light of the day shine in: light of the mind shine out!
We have a building which is more than a building.
There is a commerce between inner and outer,
between brightness and shadow,
between the world and those who think about the world.
Is it not a mystery? The parts cohere, they come together
like petals of a flower, yet they also send their tongues outward
to feel and taste the teeming earth.
Did you want classic columns and predictable pediments?
A growl of old Gothic grandeur? A blissfully boring box?
Not here, no thanks. No icon, no IKEA, no iceberg,
but curves and caverns, nooks and niches,
huddles and heavens, syncopations and surprises.
Leave symmetry to the cemetery.
But bring together slate and stainless steel,
black granite and grey granite,
seasoned oak and sycamore,
concrete blond and smooth as silk –
the mix is almost alive – it breathes and beckons –
imperial marble it is not!

Come down the Mile, into the heart of the city,
past the kirk of St Giles and the closes and wynds
of the noted ghosts of history who drank their claret
and fell down the steep tenement stairs
into the arms of link-boys
but who wrote of the starry enlightenment of their days.
And before them the auld makars
who tickled a Scottish king's ear with melody
and ribaldry and frank advice.
And when you are there, down there, in the midst of things,
not set upon an hill with your nose in the air,
this is where you know your parliament should be,
and this is where it is, just here.

What do the people want of the place?
They want it to be filled with thinking people
as open and adventurous as its architecture.
A nest of fearties is what they do not want.
A symposium of procrastinators is what they do not want.
A phalanx of forelock tuggers is what they do not want.
And perhaps above all the droopy mantra of 'it wizny me'
is what they do not want.
Dear friends, dear lawgivers, dear parliamentarians,
you are picking up a thread of pride and self-esteem
that has been almost but not quite, oh no not quite,
not ever broken or forgotten.
When you reconvene you will be reconvening
with a sense of not wholly the power,
not yet wholly the power,
but a good sense of what was once in the honour of your grasp.
All right. Forget, or don't forget, the past.
Trumpets and robes are fine,
but in the present and the future you will need something more.
What is it? We, the people, cannot tell you yet,
but you will know about it when we do tell you.
We give you our consent to govern, don't pocket it and ride away.
We give you our deepest, dearest wish to govern well,
don't say we have no mandate to be so bold.
We give you this great building,
don't let your work and hope be other than great
when you enter and begin.
So now begin. Open the doors and begin.

THE VISION OF ENRIC MIRALLES

James Robertson b.1958

A subtle game of views and implications
is what I play. Once, Edinburgh was this:
a mountain and some buildings, synthesis
of human and geological formations.
What we create must fit with what's on hand –
cut through the Old Town's grain and yet enhance,
be mindful of the past, and yet advance –
a Parliament that sits within the land,
a gathering where land and people meet.
The land itself will be a building-block:
to me this is of greatest consequence.
The Parliament will grow from Arthur's Seat,
a bridge between the city and the rock,
a mirror of the land it represents.

I think of Scotland and I think of boats.
Always these boats are present in my mind,
and by their shapes the building is defined:
a Parliament on land and yet it floats;
a set of shelters under upturned keels,
an anchorage, a point of embarkation,
a source of new light for an old dark nation,
a place of thoughts, ambitions and ideals.
But all they want to know – how much? and when?
as if the future will not pay or wait.
I tell them it will cost what it will cost,
be finished when it's finished, not till then.
Why do they only call *too dear, so late,*
that which for three whole centuries was lost?

3

BRIGHT IS THE RING OF WORDS

Robert Louis Stevenson 1850–94

Bright is the ring of words
When the right man rings them,
Fair the fall of songs
When the singer sings them.
Still they are carolled and said –
On wings they are carried –
After the singer is dead
And the maker buried.

Low as the singer lies
In the field of heather,
Songs of his fashion bring
The swains together.
And when the west is red
With the sunset embers,
The lover lingers and sings
And the maid remembers.

4

BALLADE OF THE TWEED
Andrew Lang 1844–1912

The ferox rins in rough Loch Awe,
A weary cry frae ony toun;
The Spey, that loups o'er linn and fa',
They praise a' ither streams aboon;
They boast their braes o' bonny Doon:
Gie me to hear the ringing reel,
Where shilfas sing and cushats croon
By fair Tweedside, at Ashestiel!

There's Ettrick, Megget, Ale, and a',
Where trout swim thick in May and June;
Ye'll see them take in showers o' snaw
Some blinking, cauldrife April noon:
Rax ower the palmer and march-broun,
And syne we'll show a bonny creel,
In spring or simmer, late or soon,
By fair Tweedside, at Ashestiel!

There's mony a water, great or sma',
Gaes singing in his siller tune,
Through glen and heuch, and hope and shaw,
Beneath the sunlicht or the moon:
But set us in our fishing shoon
Between the Caddon burn and Peel,
And syne we'll cross the heather broun
By fair Tweedside, at Ashestiel!

ferox: lancet fish; *shilfas*: finches; *cushats*: doves; *cauldrife*: chilly; *rax*: throw; *palmer/march-broun*: fishing lures; *heuch*: crag; *hope*: top of glen; *shaw*: grove

Envoi

Deil tak the dirty trading loon
Wad gar the water ca' his wheel,
And drift his dyes and poisons doun
By fair Tweedside, at Ashestiel!

5

SCOTLAND

Robert Crawford b.1959

Semiconductor country, land crammed with intimate expanses,
Your cities are superlattices, heterojunctive
Graphed from the air, your cropmarked farmlands
Are epitaxies of tweed.

All night motorways carry your signal, swept
To East Kibride or Dunfermline. A brightness off low headlands
Beams-in the dawn to Fife's interstices,
Optoelectronics of hay.

Micro-nation. So small you cannot be forgotten,
Bible inscribed on a ricegrain, hi-tech's key
Locked into the earth, your televised Glasgows
Are broadcast in Rio. Among circuitboard crowsteps

To be miniaturised is not small-minded.
To love you needs more detail than the Book of Kells –
Your harbours, your photography, your democratic intellect
Still boundless, chip of a nation.

6

THE FOUR MARIES

Anon

Yestreen the queen had four Maries,
The nicht she'll hae but three;
There was Mary Seaton, and Mary Beaton,
And Mary Carmichael, and me.

O often have I drest my queen,
And put gold on her hair,
But now I've gotten for my reward
The gallows to be my share.

O often have I drest my queen
And often made her bed;
But now I've gotten for my reward
The gallows-tree to tread.

I charge ye all, ye mariners,
When ye sail ower the faem,
Let neither my father nor mother get wit
That I'm not coming hame.

I charge ye all, ye mariners,
That sail upon the sea,
Let neither my father nor mother get wit
This dog's death I'm to dee.

For if my father and mother get wit
And my bold brithers three,
O meikle wad be the gude red blude
This day wad be spilt for me!

O little did my mother ken
That day she cradled me
The land I was to travel in
Or the death I was to dee.

SPEAKING OF SCOTLAND
Maurice Lindsay b.1918

What do you mean when you speak of Scotland?
The grey defeats that are dead and gone
behind the legends each generation
savours afresh, yet can't live on?

Lowland farms with their broad acres
peopling crops? The colder earth
of the North East? Or Highland mountains
shouldering up their rocky dearth?

Inheritance of guilt that our country
has never stood where we feel she should?
A nagging threat of unfinished struggle
somehow forever lost in the blood?

Scotland's a sense of change, an endless
becoming for which there was never a kind
of wholeness or ultimate category.
Scotland's an attitude of mind.

THE BONNY HOUSE O AIRLIE

Anon

It fell on a day, and a bonny simmer's day
When green grew aits and barley,
That there fell out a great dispute
Between Argyll and Airlie.

Argyll has raised a hunner men,
A hunner harnessed rarely,
And he's awa by the back o Dunkeld
To plunder the castle o Airlie.

Lady Ogilvie looks o'er her bower window,
And oh but she looks weary
When there she spies the great Argyll
Come to plunder the bonny house o Airlie.

'Come doon, come doon, my Lady Ogilvie,
Come doon and kiss me fairly.'
'O I winna kiss the fause Argyll
If he shouldna leave a standing stane in Airlie.'

He's taen her by the left shoulder,
Saying, 'Dame, where lies thy dowry?'
'O it's east and west o yon waterside
And it's doon by the banks o the Airlie.'

They hae sought it up, they hae sought it doon,
They hae sought it maist severely,
Till they fand it on the fair plum-tree
That shines on the bowling-green o Airlie.

He's taen her by the middle sae small,
And O, but she grat sairly!
And he's laid her down by the bonny burnside
Till they'd plundered the castle o Airlie.

'Gif my gude lord war here this nicht
As he is with King Chairlie,
Neither you nor ony ither Scottish lord
Durst avow to the plundering o Airlie.

'Gif my gude lord war now at hame,
As he is with his king,
There durst nae a Campbell in a' Argyll
Set fit on Airlie green.

'Ten bonny sons I have born unto him,
The eleventh ne'er saw his daddy;
But though I had a hunner mair
I'd gie them a' to King Chairlie.'

9

LORD ULLIN'S DAUGHTER
Thomas Campbell 1777–1844

A chieftain to the Highlands bound,
Cries, 'Boatman, do not tarry;
And I'll give thee a silver pound
To row us o'er the ferry.'

'Now who be ye would cross Lochgyle,
This dark and stormy water?'
'Oh, I'm the chief of Ulva's isle
And this Lord Ullin's daughter.

'And fast before her father's men
Three days we've fled together,
For should he find us in the glen,
My blood would stain the heather.

'His horsemen hard behind us ride;
Should they our steps discover,
Then who will cheer my bonny bride
When they have slain her lover?'

Out spoke the hardy Highland wight:
'I'll go, my chief – I'm ready:
It is not for your silver bright
But for your winsome lady.

'And by my word, the bonny bird
In danger shall not tarry;
So though the waves are raging white
I'll row you o'er the ferry.'

By this the storm grew loud apace,
The water-wraith was shrieking;
And in the scowl of heaven each face
Grew dark as they were speaking.

But still, as wilder grew the wind,
And as the night grew drearer,
A-down the glen rode armèd men –
Their tramping sounded nearer.

'O haste thee, haste!' the lady cries,
'Though tempests round us gather;
I'll meet the raging of the skies,
But not an angry father.'

The boat has left a stormy land,
A stormy sea before her –
When oh! too strong for human hand
The tempest gathered o'er her.

And still they rowed amidst the roar
Of waters fast prevailing;
Lord Ullin reached that fatal shore –
His wrath was changed to wailing.

For sore dismay'd, through storm and shade,
His child he did discover;
One lovely hand was stretched for aid,
And one was round her lover.

'Come back! come back!' he cried in grief,
'Across this stormy water;
And I'll forgive your Highland chief,
My daughter! – oh, my daughter!'

'Twas vain: the loud waves lashed the shore,
Return or aid preventing;
The waters wild went o'er his child,
And he was left lamenting.

10

POEM FOR MY SISTER

Liz Lochhead b.1948

My little sister likes to try my shoes,
to strut in them,
admire her spindle-thin twelve-year-old legs
in this season's styles.
She says they fit her perfectly,
but wobbles
on their high heels, they're
hard to balance.

I like to watch my little sister
playing hopscotch,
admire the neat hops-and-skips of her,
their quick peck,
never missing their mark, not
overstepping the line.
She is competent at peever.

I try to warn my little sister
about unsuitable shoes,
point out my own distorted feet, the callouses,
odd patches of hard skin.
I should not like to see her
in *my* shoes.
I wish she could stay
sure-footed,
        sensibly shod.

MY FATHER

Kirkpatrick Dobie 1908–99

My father was a man for stopping horses.
To screams and yells
preceded by a rattling rising roar
the beast appeared,
head reared,
eye rolling black-blobbed swum in white,
battering the cobbles with a bounding cart,
frenzied to freeze the heart.

But at the sight my father's spirit rose
and as the echoes rang
he ran and sprang
high at the rampant head
and bore it down;
with all of fourteen stone
muscle and bone,
hung! and hung on!

I've never visited his grave.
I couldn't stand and moralise
or seem to take his size.
What I remember doesn't lie
in any cemetery.
I have his stick
rough-handled, thick,
and now in my own wintry weather
stumble or slip
I feel his grip.

12

UNCLE

Ellie McDonald b.1937

Sam was the family embarrassment
in down-at-the-heel shoes and muffler,
exuding a faint aroma of fish and chips.
His infrequent visits were I suspect

vaguely connected with cash and failure
of yet another certainty at Newbury,
but to me they were something close
to magic – for who else could find

an ace of hearts behind my ear, or build
a house of cards that never fell?
No-one else's uncle had ever held
a whole platoon of Germans in a trench

at Passchendaele, nor played the concertina
for the Kaiser. Once he let me hold his medals,
two bronze and one silver hung from coloured
ribbon on a long gold clasp.

They too belonged to the magic time.

When he died, they scattered his ashes
from the window of an overnight sleeper
as it pounded across the Tay Bridge.
His final suspension of disbelief.

13

THE PEERIE GRANDSON

C. M. Costie 1902–67

'He's no a bonny bairn,' said sheu,
An sheu lached an lukk'd at me,
'Wae sic a muckle bleupsy face,
An peerie glinderan ee.
His lugs stick oot, an his ravsey heid's
As coorse as a burrie brae.
Na, na, he's far frae bonny,
Care I no whit folk say!'

'Bit he'll be a man at man's behave
Whin thee an me's baith deed,
An he'll be eeble teu,' I said,
'Tae win his daily breed.
A bairn that's witty, an weel, an strong
An can run, an hear, an see,
Hid maks nee odds aboot his luks,
He's a bonny bairn tae me.'

Sheu couldna see i the turn o his cheek,
The face o Jock, me man,
Nor yet i the shape o his peerie knevs
Me faither's wark-worn haan;
Sheu couldna see, as he lached tae me,
The glisk o me mither's face,
As she turned i the lowe o the baekeen fire,
Sayan, 'Bairns, noo, be apace!'

sheu: she; *lached*: laughed; *bleupsy*: blotchy; *glinderan ee*: half-open eyes; *ravsey*: tousled; *eeble teu*: able too; *peerie knevs*: wee fists; *glisk*: look; *apace*: at peace

Hoo could sheu ken that the soond o his voice
Is the marrows o een lang gane,
Echoan doon the years tae me
As I sit by the fire, alane;
Or ken that the luk o his ravsey heid,
An the feel o his thick yellow hair,
Taks a lump tae me hass for me peerie lass
Asleep i the Kirkyaird there.
Bit weel deu I ken that the Saviour o aa,
The Ga'er an Taaker o men,
His happit them aa i a bundle sma
An gaen me them back again.

the marrows o een lang gane: the likeness of one long gone; *hass*: throat;
Ga'er: Giver; *happit*: wrapped

14

A PAN DROP MAN

Raymond Vettese b.1950

My grandfaither wad hae deed for a pan drop.
He'd sook them day an' nicht
wi toothless tortoise gooms leathert
aifter mony years withooten dentures
(fickle things no warth fashin wi).
He smelt aye o peppermint, ma grandfaither,
in a suit o midnicht-blue (dooble-breisted),
wi a temper as het as cayenne
or guid spicy haggis, wi a bulge in's
chooks like a haimster's baggit wi seed
but fu in his case o yon sweets,
twa or three at a time, clickin like
boolies in a pooch as they joogled.
Whaun he deed we fund a hauf
feenisht paiket on the bedside table.
That wad hae scunnert him, nae doot;
that, for him, wad be deein afore his time.
We should hae cuist a poke o them, no yirth,
intil the grave. God wad hae smiled, shairly,
een gif yon white-faced meenister
(a pan drop face, whit a synchronistic metaphor!)
wad hae grued like ane that's juist sookit
straught aff a pund o soor plums, things
my grandfaither wadna be see deid wi,
a pan drop man aa the days o his life.

chooks: cheeks; *een gif*: even if; *grued*: shuddered

15

WAKING WITH RUSSELL
Don Paterson b.1963

Whatever the difference is, it all began
the day we woke up face-to-face like lovers
and his four-day-old smile dawned on him again,
possessed him, till it would not fall or waver;
and I pitched back not my old hard-pressed grin
but his own smile, or one I'd rediscovered.
Dear son, I was *mezzo del cammin*[1]
and the true path was as lost to me as ever
when you cut in front and lit it as you ran.
See how the true gift never leaves the giver:
returned and redelivered, it rolled on
until the smile poured through us like a river.
How fine, I thought, this waking amongst men!
I kissed your mouth and pledged myself for ever.

[1]   In the middle of the journey (Dante)

16

WALKING IN THE BOTANIC GARDENS, GLASGOW

For my sisters, Carole and Pam

Gordon Jarvie b.1941

I think about the folk that went before,
led full lives near this place but are no more.
I picture two small girls astride a brand-new, shiny trike;
one's sixty now and getting wobbly on her bike ...
The sun still shines, the clouds still race and pass,
the flowers still bloom and lovers lie upon the grass.
The traffic on Great Western Road is constant now,
and I am old and sport a wrinkled brow.

The same trees stretch their arms towards the sky;
they've kept their figures better far than I.
I watch a toddler run beside his dad;
why do they make me feel alive and glad?
Maybe because in them I'm forced to see
life's onward cycle, for – not once but twice thus far –
that toddler and his dad were me.

17

A RED, RED ROSE

Robert Burns 1759–96

O my luve's like a red, red rose,
That's newly sprung in June:
O my luve's like the melodie
That's sweetly play'd in tune.

As fair art thou, my bonny lass,
So deep in luve am I;
And I will luve thee still, my dear,
Till a' the seas gang dry.

Till a' the seas gang dry, my dear,
And the rocks melt wi' the sun
O I will luve thee still, my dear,
While the sands o' life shall run:

And fare thee weel, my only luve!
And fare thee weel a while!
And I will come again, my luve,
Though it were ten thousand mile.

18

THE CONFIRMATION

Edwin Muir 1887–1959

Yes, yours, my love, is the right human face.
I in my mind had waited for this long,
Seeing the false and searching for the true,
Then found you as a traveller finds a place
Of welcome suddenly amid the wrong
Valleys and rocks and twisting roads. But you,
What shall I call you? A fountain in a waste,
A well of water in a country dry,
Or anything that's honest and good, an eye
That makes the whole world bright. Your open heart,
Simple with giving, gives the primal deed,
The first good world, the blossom, the blowing seed,
The hearth, the steadfast land, the wandering sea,
Not beautiful or rare in every part,
But like yourself, as they were meant to be.

STRAWBERRIES

Edwin Morgan b.1920

There were never strawberries
like the ones we had
that sultry afternoon
sitting on the step
of the open french window
facing each other
your knees held in mine
the blue plates in our laps
the strawberries glistening
in the hot sunlight
we dipped them in sugar
looking at each other
not hurrying the feast
for one to come
the empty plates
laid on the stone together
with the two forks crossed
and I bent towards you
sweet in that air
in my arms
abandoned like a child
from your eager mouth
the taste of strawberries
in my memory
lean back again
let me love you

let the sun beat
on our forgetfulness
one hour of all
the heat intense
and summer lightning
on the Kilpatrick hills

let the storm wash the plates

20

MARY MORISON

Robert Burns 1759–96

O Mary, at thy window be,
It is the wish'd, the trysted hour!
Those smiles and glances let me see
That make the miser's treasure poor:
How blithely wad I bide the stoure,
A weary slave frae sun to sun;
Could I the rich reward secure,
The lovely Mary Morison.

Yestreen, when to the trembling string,
The dance gaed through the lighted ha',
To thee my fancy took its wing –
I sat, but neither heard nor saw:
Though this was fair, and that was braw,
And yon the toast of a' the town,
I sigh'd, and said, amang them a',
'Ye are na Mary Morison.'

O Mary, canst thou wreck his peace
Wha for thy sake wad gladly die?
Or canst thou break that heart of his
Wha's only faut is loving thee?
If love for love thou wilt na gie,
At least be pity on me shown;
A thought ungentle canna be
The thought o' Mary Morison.

MARY OF ARGYLL

Charles Jefferys 1807–65

I have heard the mavis singing
His love song to the morn,
I have seen the dewdrop clinging
To the rose but newly born.
But a sweeter song has cheer'd me
At the evening's gentle close,
And I've seen an eye still brighter
Than the dewdrop on the rose.
'Twas thy voice, my gentle Mary,
And thy artless winning smile,
That made this world an Eden,
Bonny Mary of Argyll.

Tho' thy voice may lose its sweetness
And thine eye its brightness too,
Tho' thy step may lack its fleetness
And thy hair its sunny hue,
Still to me wilt thou be dearer
Than all the world shall own,
I have loved thee for thy beauty
But not for that alone.
I have watched thy heart, dear Mary,
And its goodness was the wile
That has made thee mine forever,
Bonny Mary of Argyll.

ANNIE LAURIE

Lady John Scott 1810–1900

Maxwellton braes are bonnie,
Where early fa's the dew,
And it's there that Annie Laurie
Gie'd me her promise true;
Gie'd me her promise true,
That ne'er forgot shall be;
But for bonnie Annie Laurie
I'd lay doun my head and dee.

Her brow is like the snaw-drift,
Her neck is like the swan,
Her face it is the fairest
That e'er the sun shone on;
That e'er the sun shone on,
And dark blue is her e'e;
And for bonnie Annie Laurie
I'd lay doun my head and dee.

Like dew on the gowan lying
Is the fa' o' her fairy feet;
And like winds in summer sighing
Her voice is low and sweet;
Her voice is low and sweet
And she's a' the world to me,
And for bonnie Annie Laurie
I'd lay doun my head and dee.

23

LOVE SONG

Joseph Macleod ('Adam Drinan') 1903–84

Soft as the wind your hair,
gull-gleaming your breasts.
I hoard no treasure there.
I do not grope for rest.
I seek you as my home,
that all your sensitive life
may fuse into my own,
and the world match with my wife.

I carry you out of this
to no enchanted isle.
Blood is tart in your kiss,
and no dream in your smile.
Bitter, bitter the hours
and coasts of our patrol.
Foggy this Minch of ours.
But I sail with your soul.

I come to you in the flame
of a burst and broken land.
There is acid in my brain
and withering in my hand.
Your touch will plot us wise,
your quiet keep it true;
and joy be the starlight
to what we have to do.

24

LOVE IN AGE

George Bruce 1909–2002

Now that we have had our day, you
having carried, borne children,
been responsible through the wearing years,
in this moment and the next
and still the next as our love
spreads to tomorrow's horizon,
we talk a little before silence.

Let the young make up their love songs,
about which subject they are securely ignorant.
Let them look into eyes that mirror
themselves. Let them groan and ululate
their desire into a microphone. Let them
shout their proclamations over the tannoy
– a whisper is enough for us.

25

GLEN, A SHEEPDOG
Hilton Brown b.1890

I ken there isna a pint in yer heid,
I ken that ye're auld an' ill,
An' the dogs ye focht in yer day are deid,
An' I doot that ye've focht yer fill;
Ye're the dourest deevil in Lothian land,
But, man, the hert o' ye's simply grand;
Ye're done an' doited but gie's yer hand
An' we'll thole ye a whilie still.

A daft-like character aye ye've been
Sin the day I brocht ye hame,
When I bocht ye doon at the Caddens green
An' gie'd ye a guid Scots name;
Y've spiled the sheep an' ye've chased the stirk,
An' rabbits was mair tae yer mind nor work,
An' ye've left in the morn an' stopped till mirk,
But I've keepit ye a' the same.

Mebbe ye're failin' an' mebbe I'm weak,
An' there's younger dogs tae fee
But I doot that a new freen's ill tae seek,
An' I'm thinkin' I'll let them be;
Ye've whiles been richt whaur I've thocht wrang,
Ye've liked me weel an' ye've liked me lang,
An' when there's ane o' us got tae gang –
May the guid Lord mak it me.

---

pint: pint measure (of sense); *doited*: feeble; *spiled*: spoiled; *stopped*, stayed away; *fee*: hire; *whiles*: sometimes

A DUG A DUG

Bill Keys 1928–99

Hey, daddy, wid ye get us a dug?
A big broon alsatian ur a wee white pug?
Ur a skinny wee terrier ur a big fat vull?
Aw, daddy, get us a dug. Wull yi?

Whit! An' whose dug'll it be when it durties the flerr,
An' pees'n the carpet, an' messes the sterr?
It's me ur yur mammy'll be tane furra mug.
Away oot'n play. Yur no gettin a dug.

But, daddy, thur gien them away
Doon therr at the RSPCA.
Yu'll get wan fur nothing so yi wull.
Aw, daddy, get us a dug. Wull yi?

Dji hear um? Oan aboot dugs again?
Ah think that yin's goat dugs'n the brain.
Ah know whit yull get: a skite in the lug
If ah hear ony merr aboot this bliddy dug.

Ah, daddy, it widny be dear tae keep
An' ah'd make it a basket fur it tae sleep
An' ah'd take it for runs away ower the hull.
Aw, daddy, get us a dug. Wull yi?

Ah doan't think thur's ever been emdy like you:
Yi could wheedle the twist oota flamin' corkscrew.
Noo! Get doon aff mah neck. Gie's nane a yur hug.
Aw right. That's anuff. Ah'll get yi a dug.

Aw, daddy. A dug. A dug.

27

THE BLUE DOO

Jimmy Copeland 1918–2002

There was wunst a wee doo,
An' this wee doo was blue,
It had got itsel' right in a mess.
Now it might be that you
Never heard of this doo.
Well, ah'll tell ye or you'd never guess.

Well, this wee doo was seeck,
It had banjo'd its beak,
Jist wi' stabbin' a daud of stale breid.
When alang came a boy,
Jist a durrty wee boy,
Who had snotters an' beasts in his heid.

Said the wee boy – Aw jings!
Ah love a' things wi' wings!
An' he gied the wee doo a big cuddle,
Then he mended its beak,
He jist gied it a tweak,
Then he saftened its breid in a puddle.

Well, the doo gulped the breid,
It wiz hunger – no' greed,
An' it said tae the boy – Thanksalo',
For yir jist a wee pe'
An' ah'll never forge',
End the truth is it nevah forgot![1]

---

[1] This line is to be read in a posh voice

So youse people take heed,
Ayeways saften doos' breid,
An' never smack boys who have beasts in their heid,
For ye might smack the boy
Who was good to the doo,
An' the next thing ye'll know is –
The doo might get you!

28

THE WEE COCK SPARRA

Duncan Macrae 1905–67
and Hugh Frater

A wee cock sparra sat on a tree,
A wee cock sparra sat on a tree,
A wee cock sparra sat on a tree,
Chirpin awa as blithe as could be.

Alang came a boy wi' a bow and an arra,
Alang came a boy wi' a bow and an arra,
Alang came a boy wi' a bow and an arra,
And he said: 'I'll get ye, ye wee cock sparra.'

The boy wi' the arra let fly at the sparra,
The boy wi' the arra let fly at the sparra,
The boy wi' the arra let fly at the sparra,
And he hit a man that was hurlin' a barra.

The man wi' the barra came owre wi' the arra,
The man wi' the barra came owre wi' the arra,
The man wi' the barra came owre wi' the arra,
And said: 'Ye take me for a wee cock sparra?'

The man hit the boy, tho he wasne his farra,
The man hit the boy, tho he wasne his farra,
The man hit the boy, tho he wasne his farra,
And the boy stood and glowered; he was hurt tae the marra.

And a' this time the wee cock sparra,
And a' this time the wee cock sparra,
And a' this time the wee cock sparra,
Was chirpin awa on the shank o' the barra.

THREE CRAWS

Anon

Three craws sat upon a wa,
Sat upon a wa, sat upon a wa,
Three craws sat upon a wa
On a cauld an frosty mornin.

The first craw was greetin fur his maw,
Greetin fur his maw, greetin fur his maw,
The first craw was greetin fur his maw
On a cauld an frosty mornin.

The second craw fell an brak his jaw,
Fell an brak his jaw, fell an brak his jaw,
The second craw fell an brak his jaw
On a cauld an frosty mornin.

The third craw couldnae caw at a,
Couldnae caw at a, couldnae caw at a,
The third craw couldnae caw at a
On a cauld an frosty mornin.

An that's a, absolutely a,
Absolutely a, absolutely a,
An that's a, absolutely a
On a cauld an frosty mornin.

30

THE PARROT: A TRUE STORY

Thomas Campbell 1777–1844

A parrot, from the Spanish Main,
Full young and early caged, came o'er,
With bright wings, to the bleak domain
Of Mulla's shore.

To spicy groves where he had won
His plumage of resplendent hue,
His native fruits, and skies, and sun,
He bade adieu.

For these he exchanged the smoke of turf,
A heathery land and misty sky,
And turned on rocks and raging surf
His golden eye.

But petted in our climate cold
He lived and chattered many a day:
Until with age, from green and gold
His wings grew grey.

At last when blind, and seeming dumb,
He scolded, laughed and spoke no more,
A Spanish stranger chanced to come
To Mulla's shore.

He hailed the bird in Spanish speech,
The bird in Spanish speech replied;
Flapped round the cage with joyous screech,
Dropt down, and died.

Mulla: Mull

31

THE TALE OF A FISH
Jimmy Copeland 1918–2002

A skavvy once delved in
A stank near the Kelvin,
When he heard a big splash in the watter,
He thought he was dreamin',
For a salmon, a' gleamin',
Had loupt an' lunged back wi' a clatter.

Well, the skavvy near fell,
An' he said to himsel',
Did I see what my ears have just saw?
But I have to explain
He was pure Highland strain,
And he wished he was back at Loch Awe.

So he eyed up the fish,
Ah, but not as a dish!
It was more like a meeting of souls,
There was no thought of food,
For this skavvy was good,
An' forbye he had mince in his rolls.

He said – everyone knows
That the salmon-kind goes
From the stream to the ocean and back,
But the Kelvin that was
Is long vanished because
What was crystal is bloody near black.

It's the sludge and the slops
From the factories and shops,
For what do the industries care?
And between you and me
there's the great BBC,
And you know what they pour out from there!

You're the king of the river,
But, man, will you ever
Win back to the redds of your home?
Yet you leap and you dive,
And you struggle and strive
As the call brings you back from the foam.

In my own sorry life
I'm no stranger to strife
As I delve for my wages in muck,
There's escape that I seek
With my coupon each week,
And I'm praying I'll yet have the luck.

We're a man and a fish
With the same yearning wish,
But I'm thinking we're two sorry fools,
For there's me and there's you
And the things we go through
While we're hoping we'll each win the pools.

HERON

J. K. Annand 1908–93

A humphy-backit heron
Nearly as big as me
Stands at the waterside
Fishin for his tea.
His skinny-ma-linkie lang legs
Juist like reeds
Cheats aa the puddocks
Soomin' mang the weeds.
Here's ane comin,
Grup it by the leg!
It sticks in his thrapple
Then slides doun his craig.
Neist comes a rottan,
A rottan soomin past,
Oot gangs the lang neb
And has the rottan fast.
He jabs it, he stabs it,
Sune it's in his wame,
Flip-flap in the air
Heron flees hame.

puddock: frog; *rottan*: rat; *wame*: belly

MY LAST WORD ON FROGS
Norman MacCaig 1910–96

People have said to me, *You seem to like frogs.*
They keep jumping into your poems.

I do. I love the way they sit,
compact as a cat and as indifferent
to everything but style, like a lady remembering
to keep her knees together. And I love
the elegant way they jump and
the inelegant way they land.
So human.

I feel so close to them
I must be froggish myself.
I look in the mirror expecting to see
a fairytale Prince.

But no. It's just sprawling me,
croaking away
and swivelling my eyes around
for the stealthy heron and his stabbing beak.

THE WEE KIRKCUDBRIGHT CENTIPEDE
Matt McGinn 1928–77

The Wee Kirkcudbright Centipede
She was very sweet,
She was ever so proud of every
One of her hundred feet.
Early every morning,
Her neighbours came to glance,
She always entertained them
With a beautiful little dance.

Chorus
As leg number ninety-four
Gave ninety-five a shunt,
Legs number one and two
Were twistin' out in front,
As legs number nine and ten
Were wriggling up the side,
Legs seventy-three and seventy-four
Were doing the Palais Glide.

Her neighbour Jenny Longlegs
With jealousy was mad,
She went out and bought herself
A pencil and a pad.
She came a month of mornings
And made a careful note
Of every step the centipede made
And this is what she wrote.

Armed with exact notation,
Young Jenny Longlegs tried
To dance just like the centipede,
She failed and nearly cried.
She grabbed hold of the centipede,
She says, 'Now have a look
And tell me how you do these steps
I've written in my book?'

Said the centipede, 'Do I do that?'
And she tried to demonstrate,
She'd never thought on the thing before,
She got into a terrible state,
Her hundred legs were twisted,
She got tied up in a fankle,
She fractured seven shinbones,
Fourteen kneecaps and an ankle.

As legs number one and two
Were tied to three and four,
Legs number five and six
Were trampled on the floor,
Leg number fifteen
Was attacked by number ten,
And ninety-seven and ninety-eight
Will never dance again.

The Wee Kirkcudbright Centipede,
She suffered terrible pain,
And some of us were quite surprised
She ever danced again.
But now she tells her neighbours,
Every one that calls to see,
Never try an explanation
Of what comes naturally.

THE FOX'S SKIN

Marion Angus 1854–1944

When the wark's aw dune and the world's aw still,
And whaups are swoopin across the hill,
And mither stands cryin, 'Bairns, come ben,'
It's time for the Hame o the Pictish Men.

A sorrowful wind gaes up an doon,
An me my lane in the licht o the moon,
Gaitherin a bunch o the floorin whin,
Wi ma auld fur collar hapt roond ma chin.

A star is shining on Morven Glen –
It shines on the Hame o the Pictish Men.
Hither and yont their dust is gane,
But ane o them's keekin ahint yon stane.

His queer auld face is wrinkled an riven,
Like a raggedy leaf, sae drookit an driven.
There's nocht to be feared at his ancient ways,
For this is aw that iver he says:

'The same auld wind at its weary cry:
The blin-faced moon in the misty sky;
A thoosand years o clood an flame,
An aw things the same an aye the same –
The lass is the same in the fox's skin,
Gaitherin the bloom o the floorin whin.'

---

whaups: curlews; *my lane*: alone; *floorin*: flowering; *hapt*: wrapped

THE FIRST HOOLIT'S PRAYER

Ian McFadyen

'Ah'll tak the nicht-shift,' says the hoolit.
'The nicht-shift suits me fine –
An i' the deeps o winter
Ah'll aye dae the overtime.

'Dinna send me wi thae ithir birds
cheepin in a choir
i the gloamin or at brek o day
lined up oan a wire.

'But gie tae me a solo pairt,
markin oot the nicht
wi low notes that gie goose-pricks
an hie anes that gie frichts.

'An Lord, dinna pey me
wi nuts or crumbs or seeds:
Ah want tae be carniverous
an chow aff rottans' heids.

hoolit: owl; *rottans'*: rats'

37

AIKEN DRUM

Anon

There came a man tae oor toun,
Tae oor toon, tae oor toon,
O a strange man came tae oor toon
And they ca'd him Aiken Drum.

> *Chorus*
> *And he played upon a ladle,*
> *A ladle, a ladle,*
> *And he played upon a ladle*
> *And his name was Aiken Drum.*

O his coat wis made o the guid roast beef,
O the guid roast beef, o the guid roast beef,
O his coat wis made o the guid roast beef
And his name was Aiken Drum.

And his breeks were made o haggis bags,
O haggis bags, o haggis bags,
And his breeks were made o haggis bags
And his name was Aiken Drum.

And his buttons were made o bawbee baps,
O bawbee baps, o bawbee baps,
And his buttons were made o bawbee baps
And his name was Aiken Drum.

bawbee baps: penny rolls

38

THE TRAIN TO GLASGOW

Wilma Horsbrugh 1903–95

Here is the train to Glasgow.
Here is the driver,
Mr MacIver,
Who drove the train to Glasgow.
Here is the guard from Donibristle
Who waved his flag and blew his whistle
To tell the driver,
Mr MacIver,
To start the train to Glasgow.

Here is a boy called Donald MacBrane
Who came to the station to catch the train
But saw the guard from Donibristle
Wave his flag and blow his whistle
To tell the driver,
Mr MacIver,
To start the train to Glasgow.

Here is the guard, a kindly man
Who, at the last moment, hauled into the van
That fortunate boy called Donald MacBrane
Who came to the station to catch the train
But saw the guard from Donibristle
Wave his flag and blow his whistle
To tell the driver,
Mr MacIver,
To start the train to Glasgow.

Here are the hens and here are the cocks,
Clucking and crowing inside their box,
In charge of the guard, that kindly man
Who, at the last moment, hauled into the van
That fortunate boy called Donald MacBrane
Who came to the station to catch the train
But saw the guard from Donibristle
Wave his flag and blow his whistle
To tell the driver,
Mr MacIver,
To start the train to Glasgow.

Here is the train. It gave a jolt
Which loosened a catch and loosened a bolt,
And let out the hens and let out the cocks,
Clucking and crowing out of their box,
In charge of the guard, that kindly man
Who, at the last moment, hauled into the van
That fortunate boy called Donald MacBrane
Who came to the station to catch the train
But saw the guard from Donibristle
Wave his flag and blow his whistle
To tell the driver,
Mr MacIver,
To start the train to Glasgow.

The guard chased a hen and, missing it, fell.
The hens were all squawking (and the cocks as well).
And unless you were there you haven't a notion
Of the flurry and fuss, the noise and commotion
Caused by the train when it gave a jolt
And loosened a catch and loosened a bolt
And let out the hens and let out the cocks,
Clucking and crowing out of their box,
In charge of the guard, that kindly man
Who, at the last moment, hauled into the van
That fortunate boy called Donald MacBrane
Who came to the station to catch the train
But saw the guard from Donibristle
Wave his flag and blow his whistle
To tell the driver,
Mr MacIver,
To start the train to Glasgow.

Now Donald was quick and Donald was neat
And Donald was nimble on his feet.
He caught the hens and he caught the cocks
And he put them back in their big box.
The guard was pleased as pleased could be
And invited Donald to come to tea
On Saturday, at Donibristle,
And let him blow his guardsman's whistle
And said in all his life he'd never
Seen a boy so quick and clever,
And so did the driver,
Mr MacIver,
Who drove the train to Glasgow.

THE TAY BRIDGE DISASTER
William McGonagall c.1825–1902

Beautiful Railway Bridge of the Silv'ry Tay!
Alas! I am very sorry to say
That ninety lives have been taken away
On the last Sabbath day of 1879,
Which will be remember'd for a very long time.

'Twas about seven o'clock at night,
And the wind it blew with all its might,
And the rain came pouring down,
And the dark clouds seem'd to frown,
And the Demon of the air seem'd to say –
'I'll blow down the Bridge of Tay.'

When the train left Edinburgh
The passengers' hearts were light and felt no sorrow,
But Boreas blew a terrific gale,
Which made their hearts for to quail,
And many of the passengers with fear did say –
'I hope God will send us safe across the Bridge of Tay.'

But when the train came near to Wormit Bay,
Boreas he did loud and angry bray,
And shook the central girders of the Bridge of Tay
On the last Sabbath day of 1879,
Which will be remember'd for a very long time.

So the train sped on with all its might,
And Bonnie Dundee soon hove into sight,
And the passengers' hearts felt light,
Thinking they would enjoy Old Year's Night
With their friends at home they lov'd most dear,
And wish them all a Happy New Year.

So the train mov'd slowly along the Bridge of Tay
Until it was about midway.
Then the central girders with a crash gave way,
And down went train and passengers into the Tay!
The Storm Fiend did loudly bray,
Because ninety lives had been taken away,
On the last Sabbath day of 1879,
Which will be remember'd for a very long time.

As soon as the catastrophe came to be known
The alarm from mouth to mouth was blown,
And the cry rang out all o'er the town,
Good Heavens! The Tay Bridge is blown down,
And a passenger train from Edinburgh –
Which fill'd all the people's hearts with sorrow,
And made them for to turn pale,
Because none of the passengers had liv'd to tell the tale
How the disaster happen'd on the last Sabbath day of 1879,
Which will be remember'd for a very long time.

It must have been an awful sight
To witness all this by dusky moonlight,
While the Storm Fiend did laugh, and angry did bray,
Along the Railway Bridge of the Silv'ry Tay.
Oh! ill-fated Bridge of the Silv'ry Tay,
I must now conclude my lay
By telling the world fearlessly without the least dismay,
That your central girders would not have given way,
Or so do many sensible people confess,
Had they been supported at each side with buttresses.
For the stronger we our houses do build,
The less chance we have of being killed.

40

THE BOY ON THE TRAIN

M. C. Smith 1869–1938

Whit wey does the engine say *Toot-toot*?
Is it feart to gang in the tunnel?
Whit wey is the furnace no pit oot
When the rain runs doon the funnel?
What'll I hae for my tea the nicht?
A herrin' or maybe a haddie?
Has Gran'ma gotten electric licht?
Is the next stop Kirkcaddy?

There's a hoodie-craw on yon turnips raw!
An seagulls – sax or seeven.
I'll no fa' oot the windae, Maw,
It's sneckit as sure as I'm leevin'.
We're into the tunnel, we're aw in the dark!
But dinnae be frichtit, Daddy,
We'll sune be comin' to Beveridge Park,
And the next stop's Kirkcaddy.

Is yon the mune I see in the sky?
It's awfie wee an curly,
See, there's a coo an a cauf ootbye,
An a lassie pu'in a hurly!
He's chackit the tickets and gien them back,
Sae gie me my ain yin, Daddy,
Lift doon the bag frae the luggage rack,
For the next stop's Kirkcaddy.

leevin': living

There's a gey wheen boats at the harbour mou',
And eh! dae ya see the cruisers?
The cinnamon drop I was sookin' the noo
Has tummelt an stuck tae ma troosers ...
I'll sune be ringin' ma Gran'ma's bell,
She'll cry, 'Come ben, my laddie,'
For I ken mysel by the queer-like smell
That the next stop's Kirkcaddy!

41

THE POACHER TO ORION

Violet Jacob 1863–1946

November-month is wearin by,
The leaves is nearly doon;
I watch ye stride alang the sky
O nichts, my beltit loon.

The treetaps wi their fingers bare
Spread between me and you,
But weel in yonder frosty air
Ye see me keekin through.

At schule I lairnd richt wearilie
The Hunter was yer name;
Sma pleasure were ye then tae me,
But noo oor trade's the same.

But ye've a brawer job nor mine
And better luck nor me,
For them that sees ye likes ye fine
And the pollis lets ye be.

We're baith astir when men's asleep;
A hunter aye pursued,
I hae by dyke an ditch tae creep,
But ye gang safe an prood.

beltit loon: belted boy; *brawer*: finer; *nor*: than; *pollis*: police

What maitter that? I'll no complain,
For when we twa are met
We hae the nicht-watch for oor ain
Till the stars are like tae set.

Gang on, my lad. The warlds owreheid
Wheel on their nichtly beat,
And ye'll mind ye as the skies ye treid
O the brither at yer feet.

42

WEE DAVIE DAYLICHT

James Robertson b.1958

Wee Davie Daylicht keeks ower the hill,
Slides doon the slates and sits on the sill;
Waukens up the birdies and sets them aw tae sing:
Wee Davy Daylicht's as gallus as a king.

Wee Davy Daylicht breeshles through the toun,
Blaws oot the stars, and turns the darkness doon;
Winks in aw the windaes, shines on the stanes,
Polishes yer glesses and warms up yer banes.

Wee Davy Daylicht jinks amang the trees,
Mairches doon the High Street and flichters in the breeze.
He aye wants tae laugh, but he disna ken why –
Wee Davy Daylicht has a smile that fills the sky.

Adapted by James Robertson fae an original poem by Robert Tennant
(1830–79).

43

BLETHERTOUN ROVERS
Matthew Fitt b.1968

Blethertoun Rovers play in blue
But they havenae got a clue.
Jist last Sunday oot they ran
And got banjaxed fifteen–wan.

Their striker's name is Magnus Shore,
Couldn't hit a coo-shed door.
Last week he got the baw and spooned it –
Even noo, they havenae foond it.

The left back has them aw in fits
When he forgets his fitbaw bitts.
If he cannae get the skipper's,
He plays in the groondsman's slippers.

Jooglie the goalie lowps and rolls,
Bields the Blethertouners' goals.
Where the baw is he jist guesses
Through his muckle jam-jar glesses.

The Rovers fans are never singin,
The coach's heid is ayewise hingin.
His team are sic a bunch o duddies –
He should hae signed eleven cuddies.

Bields: Protects

44

THE COOPER O FIFE

Anon

There was a wee cooper who lived in Fife,
 Nickety-nackety noo noo noo,
And he has gotten a gentle wife;
 Hey Willie Wallachy!
 How John Dougal alane,
 Quo Rushety roo roo roo!

She wadna bake and she wadna brew,
 Nickety-nackety ...
For spoiling of her comely hue.
 Hey Willie Wallachy ...

She wadna card, she wadna spin,
For shaming o her gentle kin.

She wadna wash, she wadna wring,
For spoiling o her gowden ring.

The cooper's awa to his wool pack,
He's laid a sheepskin on his wife's back.

'I wadna thrash ye for your proud kin,
But I *will* thrash my ain sheepskin.'

'Oh I will bake and brew and spin,
And think not of my gentle kin.'

All ye who have a gentle wife,
Keep weel in mind the cooper o Fife.

45

THE BIGGERS
David C. Purdie

We are the biggers, puir buggers,
the lads that pits ruifs owre yer heids:
we're brickies an jyners an sclaters,
an plumbers an penters an spreids;
we're drivers o dumpers an heist men,
cley-davies an humphers o hudds,
we're dargers an daft barriegadgies,
in wellies an glaury auld duds.

We are the biggers, puir buggers,
that shivs up yer ceilins an waas,
ti keep yer heid dry when it's rainin
an keep yer erse warm when it snaas.
Tap taes alang scaffoldin battens
or doun i the grun howkin pitts,
wi the stour o cement an o timmer
in wir sweit an wir bluid an wir spits.

We are the biggers, puir buggers,
that pits the flairs unner yer feet;
wha tyauve in aa wins an aa wathers,
in the het an the cauld an the weet.
They artichokes, drauchtsmen an siclike
micht craw that *they've* biggit yer hame.
But dinna tak tent o thae buggers –
it's the biggers that bigg't it – no thaim!

---

dargers: workers; *barriegadgies*: smart fellows; *tyauve*: strive

THE BALLAD OF JANITOR MACKAY

Margaret Green

I wis playin keepie uppie
in the street ootside the schule,
when Jock McCann's big brither
who's an idjit an a fule,

went an tuk ma fitba aff me
an he dunted it too haud
an it stoated ower the railins
inty the janny's yard.

Aw, MacKay's a mean auld scunner.
He wis dossin in the sun,
an when my fitba pit wan oan him
big McCann beganty run,

an MacKay picked up ma fitba
an he looked at me an glowered
But I stood ma groond, fur naebody
will say that I'm a coward.

But when he lowped the palins
an he fell an skint his nose
I tukty me heels an beltit
right up ma granny's close.

I could feel the sterrwell shakin
as efter me he tore,
an he nearly cracked his wallies
as he cursed at me an swore.

'O save me gran,' I stuttered
as I reached ma granny's hoose,
fur MacKay wis gettin nearer
an his face wis turnin puce.

Noo, my gran wis hivin tea
wi Effie Bruce an Mrs Scobie,
an when she heard the stushie
she cam beltin through the loabie.

My gran is only fower fit ten
but she kens whit she's aboot.
'Ye've hud it noo, MacKay,' I cried,
'My gran will sort ye oot!'

See that janny? See ma granny?
Ma granny hit um wi a sanny,
then she timmed the bucket owerum
an he tummelt doon the sterr
an he landed in the dunny
wi the bakie in his herr.

Fortune changes awfy sudden –
imagine he cried *me* a midden!

(I goat ma ba back but.)

stushie: hullabaloo; *loabie*: hallway, lobby; *sanny*: trainer; *timmed*: emptied;
dunny: basement; *baikie*: ashes or rubbish

47

PRIMARY SCHOOL CONCERT

R. S. Richard 1943–89

These faces never really change,
standing in uneven rows staring out
from the stage,
the oval-headed, the moon-faced,
skinny or squint,
the bright-eyed boys and starry-eyed girls,
the dreamers and the dreamed of,
each in his own world.
All time does is to expand the outward shapes
but inside has been set to shape the years.
Now and Then themselves are shaped.
Run your finger over the old photograph,
the familiar bumps and gropings, the fists
in the face,
the salty tears and sticky laughter,
the wee mums in frocks, the poets in themselves,
and the wild-eyed wife-bashers.
And them looking out to the audience trying to
catch their reflections, who's reflected in whom?
Some smiling, secured in recognition, some blank,
lost upon a dark sea of unknown faces,
already wrecked.

48

THE QUALIFICATION

Tom Leonard b.1944

wurk aw yir life
nuthnty show
pit oanthi nyuze
same awl drivl

yoonyin bashn
wurkir bashn
lord this
sir soan soa thaht

shood hearma boay
sayzwi need gunz
an armd revalooshn
nuthn else wurks

awright fur him thoa
uppit thi yooni
tok aw yi like therr
that's whit its fur

49

SONGS OF THE SCOTTISH EXAM BOARD ENGLISH MARKER

William Hershaw b.1957

I

The High Schools, Academies, Colleges, Saints,
I shuffle them between my hands.

Morgan, Madras, Kelvinside, Wester Hailes,
I red ink their mistakes.

Dalbeattie, Lochgelly, Our Lady's, Balfron,
I envelope, number and grade.

Selkirk, Dalziel, Balweary, Nairn,
I process their thoughts, dreams and lives.

So many lives pass before my eyes
on the way to the rest of theirs
while mine stops here with this slow and painful business.

Through the small glass square in my attic roof
the sound of children's laughter in the street
upsets my penning rhythm.

I lift up my head in the summer heat then,
Hazelhead, Sandwick, St Columba's, Arbroath,
Royal High, Bannockburn, Dalkeith.

No future 'A' pass Higher here:
she wrote of her father and feelings,
how he lay on a waterbed
whey-faced and skeletal from fighting the cancer
the last time her mother had taken her
to the hospice for the dying.

I wrote on it:
gives a clear account of a personal experience;
communicates a sense of involvement;
sentences accurate but not varied;
does not demonstrate skill with language
or overall distinction of Credit English;
General, Grade 3.

O God,
when my final examination comes,
do not measure me
by the same pitiless criteria.

LISTEN TAE THE TEACHER

Nancy Nicolson

He's five year auld, he's aff tae school,
Fairmer's bairn, wi a pencil an a rule,
His teacher scoffs when he says 'hoose',
'The word is "house", you silly little goose.'
He tells his Ma when he gets back
He saw a 'mouse' in an auld cairt track.
His father laughs fae the stack-yard dyke,
'Yon's a "moose", ye daft wee tyke.'

> *Listen tae the teacher, dinna say dinna,*
> *Listen tae the teacher, dinna say hoose,*
> *Listen tae the teacher, ye canna say maunna,*
> *Listen tae the teacher, ye maunna say moose.*

He bit his lip and shut his mooth,
Which wan could he trust for truth?
He took his burden ower the hill
Tae auld grey Geordie o the mill.
'An did they mock thee for thy tongue,
Wi them sae auld and thoo sae young?
They werena makkin a fuil o thee,
Makkin a fuil o themsels, ye see.'

> *Listen tae the teacher ...*

Say 'hoose' tae the faither, 'house' tae the teacher,
'Moose' tae the fairmer, 'mouse' tae the preacher,
When ye're young it's well for you
Tae dae in Rome as Romans do,
But when ye grow and ye are auld
Ye needna dae as ye are tauld,
Nor trim yer tongue tae please yon dame
That scorns the language o her hame.

Listen tae the teacher ...

Then teacher thought that he wis fine,
He kept in step, he stayed in line,
An faither said that he wis gran,
Spak his ain tongue like a man.
And when he grew and made his choice
He chose his Scots, his native voice.
And I charge ye tae dae likewise
An spurn yon poor misguided cries.

Listen tae the teacher ...

51

KIDSPOEM/BAIRNSANG

Liz Lochhead b.1947

it wis January
and a gey dreich day
the first day Ah went to the school
so ma Mum happed me up in ma
good navy-blue napp coat wi the rid tartan hood
birled a scarf aroon ma neck
pu'ed on ma pixie an' ma pawkies
it wis that bitter
said *noo ye'll no starve*
gie'd me a wee kiss and a kid-on skelp oan the bum
and sent me aff across the playground
tae the place where Ah'd learn to say
it was January
and a really dismal day
the first day I went to school
so my mother wrapped me up in my
best navy-blue top coat with the red tartan hood,
twirled a scarf around my neck,
pulled on my bobble-hat and mittens
it was so bitterly cold
said *now you won't freeze to death*
gave me a little kiss and a pretend slap on the bottom
and sent me off across the playground
to the place I'd learn to forget to say

it wis January
and a gey dreich day
the first day Ah went tae the school
so ma Mum happed me up in ma
good navy-blue napp coat wi the rid tartan hood,
birled a scarf aroon ma neck,
pu'd on ma pixie and ma pawkies
it wis that bitter.

Oh saying it was one thing
but when it came to writing it
in black and white
the way it had to be said
was as if you were posh, grown-up, male, English and dead.

PARENTS' NIGHT
William Hershaw b.1957

I

Only two appointments left
and I'm not looking forward to the next
if their son is anything to go by.

Insolent, arrogant and lazy. A permanent sneer
on a truculent face you'd want to punch.

But it's the mother on her own:
she's taken time off her work to see me.
Harassed and sairly-trauchled in a cheap rain-coat,
she scrubs floors to buy the wee bastard trainers.

She must think I'm a doctor or a priest
because I get the family history;
how Dad buggered off,
how she cannae dae a thing wi the laddy.

I hivnae the hert tae tell her
and nae doubt she kens hersel.

'He's doing fine, a nice lad,
mibbe he could read a bit more at home
to improve his English ...'

2

The best pupil in the class –
a wee, quiet, mousy lassie.
Her mother, a primary teacher,
a nervous bird, pecking at my words,
feverish with poisoned thoughts.

Father puts his glasses on
(hung on a thin chain round his neck)
to read out his prepared list;
Why only a B in Higher English yet A's elsewhere?
Why no Shakespeare on the syllabus?
More practice needed with past papers, surely?
Why not more work corrected?

And I'm thinking that in half an hour
I'll be home to see my own two ...

and tomorrow I get to teach.

OLD TONGUE
Jackie Kay b.1961

When I was eight, I was forced south.
Not long after, when I opened
my mouth, a strange thing happened.
I lost my Scottish accent.
Words fell off my tongue:
eedyit, dreich, wabbit, crabbit,
stummer, teuchter, heidbanger,
so you are, so am ur, see you, see ma ma,
shut yer geggie or I'll gie ye the malkie!

My own vowels started to stretch like my bones
and I turned my back on Scotland.
Words disappeared in the dead of night,
new words marched in: ghastly, awful,
quite dreadful, scones said like stones.
Pokey hats into ice-cream cones.
Oh where did all my words go –
my old words, my lost words?
Did you ever feel sad when you lost a word,
did you ever try to call it back
like calling in the sea?
If I could have found my words wandering,
I swear I would have taken them in,
swallowed them whole, knocked them back.

Out in the English soil, my old words
buried themselves. It made my mother's blood boil.
I cried one day with the wrong sound in my mouth.
I wanted them back; I wanted my old accent back,
my old tongue. My dour, soor Scottish tongue.
Sing-songy. *I wanted to gie it laldie.*

54

STREET TALK

J. K. Annand 1908–93

There was a rammie in the street,
A stishie and stramash.
The crabbit wifie up the stair
Pit up her winda sash.

'Nou, what's adae?' the wifie cried,
'Juist tell me what's adae?'
A day is twinty-fower hours, missis,
Nou gie us peace to play.

'Juist tell me what's ado,' she cried,
'And nane o yer gab,' cried she.
D'ye no ken a doo's a pigeon, missis?
Nou haud yer wheesht a wee.

'I want to ken what's up,' she cried,
'And nae mair o yer cheek, ye loun.'
It's only yer winda that's up, missis.
For guidsake pit it doun.

55

from UNRELATED INCIDENTS (No. 6)
Tom Leonard b.1944

its aw thi
fault a
thi unions hi
said n thi
wurkirs beein
too greedy
hi added n
thi commies n
no inuff
moderates stonnin
upn gettin
coontid n
lame ducks gitn
whut huvyi
bailt oot n
white elifints
getn selt doon
thi river n

a mean
wiv goat tay
puhll in
wur belts n
wur bax ur
tay thi waw
yiv goat tay
admit it.
then hi took
ootiz nummer
eight n
geen a luvvly
wee chip up
right
biside thi flag
n tapptit doon
furra three:

a burdie.

TO A MOUNTAIN DAISY

On turning one down with the plough in April 1786
Robert Burns 1759–96

Wee, modest, crimson-tippèd flow'r,
Thou's met me in an evil hour;
For I maun crush amang the stoure
    Thy slender stem:
To spare thee now is past my pow'r,
    Thou bonnie gem.

Alas! it's no thy neebor sweet,
The bonnie lark, companion meet,
Bending thee 'mang the dewy weet,
    Wi' spreckl'd breast,
When upward-springing, blythe to greet
    The purpling east.

Cauld blew the bitter-biting north
Upon thy early, humble birth;
Yet cheerfully thou glinted forth
    Amid the storm,
Scarce rear'd above the parent earth
    Thy tender form.

The flaunting flow'rs our gardens yield,
High sheltering woods and wa's maun shield;
But thou, beneath the random bield
    O cold or stane,
Adorns the histie stibble-field,
    Unseen, alane.

There, in thy scanty mantle clad,
Thy snawy bosom sun-ward spread,
Thou lifts thy unassuming head
    In humble guise;
But now the share uptears thy bed,
    And low thou lies!

Such is the fate of artless maid,
Sweet flowret of the rural shade!
By love's simplicity betray'd,
    And guileless trust,
Till she, like thee, all soil'd, is laid
    Low i' the dust.

Such is the fate of simple bard,
On life's rough ocean luckless starr'd!
Unskilful he to note the card
    Of prudent lore,
Till billows rage, and gales blow hard,
    And whelm him o'er!

Such fate to suffering worth is giv'n,
Who long with wants and woes has striv'n,
By human pride or cunning driv'n
    To mis'ry's brink,
Till, wrench'd of ev'ry stay but Heav'n,
    He, ruin'd, sink!

---

bield: shelter; *histie*: barren; *share*: ploughshare

Ev'n thou who mourn'st the Daisy's fate,
That fate is thine – no distant date;
Stern Ruin's ploughshare drives, elate,
    Full on thy bloom,
Till, crush'd beneath the furrow's weight,
    Shall be thy doom!

57

HIGHLAND LANDSCAPE

Douglas J. Fraser 1910–96

Here, there is beauty every sense can share
Against the moving backcloth of the sky;
The murmur of the stream, the scented air,
The various enchantments for the eye.
About my feet the moor is yellow-starred
With tormentil, the friendliest of flowers;
Above, the mighty peak that stands on guard
Forms and dissolves between the passing showers.
Wherever near or far the eye may dwell,
All things contribute to a sense of fitness
So integral, it would be hard to tell
Which of them bears the more impressive witness –
The splendid sweep of the enclosing hill,
The neat perfection of the tormentil.

58

I SHALL LEAVE TONIGHT FROM EUSTON

Anon

I shall leave tonight from Euston
By the seven-thirty train,
And from Perth in the early morning
I shall see the hills again.
From the top of Ben Macdhui
I shall watch the gathering storm,
And see the crisp snow lying
At the back of Cairngorm.
I shall feel the mist from Bhrotain
And pass by Lairig Ghru
To look on dark Loch Einich
From the heights of Sgoran Dubh.
From the broken Barns of Bynack
I shall see the sunrise gleam
On the forehead of Ben Rinnes
And Strathspey awake from dream.
And again in the dusk of evening
I shall find once more alone
The dark water of the Green Loch
And the pass beyond Ryvoan.
For tonight I leave from Euston
And leave the world behind;
Who has the hills for a lover
Will find them wondrous kind.

LOCHNAGAR

Lord Byron 1788–1824

Away, ye gay landscapes, ye gardens of roses,
In you let the minions of luxury rove,
Restore me the rocks where the snow-flake reposes,
Though still they are sacred to freedom and love.
Yet Caledonia, beloved are thy mountains,
Round their white summits though elements war,
Though cataracts foam 'stead of smooth-flowing fountains,
I sigh for the valley of dark Lochnagar.

Ah! there my young footsteps in infancy wander'd,
My cap was the bonnet, my cloak was the plaid.
On chieftains long perish'd my memory ponder'd
As daily I strode through the pine-cover'd glade.
I sought not my home till the day's dying glory
Gave place to the rays of the bright polar star,
For fancy was cheer'd by traditional story
Disclos'd by the natives of dark Lochnagar!

Shades of the dead! Have I not heard your voices
Rise on the night-rolling breath of the gale?
Surely the soul of the hero rejoices,
And rides on the wind o'er his own Highland vale.
Round Lochnagar while the stormy mist gathers,
Winter presides in his cold icy car.
Clouds there encircle the forms of my fathers;
They dwell in the tempests of dark Lochnagar.

Ill-starr'd though brave, did no vision's foreboding
Tell you that fate had forsaken your cause?
Ah! were you destined to die at Culloden,
Victory crowned not your fall with applause.
Still were you happy in death's earthly slumber,
You rest with your clan in the caves of Braemar.
The pibroch resounds to the piper's loud number
Your deeds on the echoes of dark Lochnagar.

Years have roll'd on, Lochnagar, since I left you!
Years must elapse ere I tread you again.
Nature of verdure and flowers has bereft you,
Yet still are you dearer than Albion's plain.
England! thy beauties are tame and domestic
To one who has roved over mountains afar –
Oh! for the crags that are wild and majestic,
The steep frowning glories of dark Lochnagar.

60

THE ONLY BLOODY HILL IN SCOTLAND
Sheena Blackhall b.1947

Ten summers young. The day, all heat on heather.
The purple pathway brittle underfoot,
The peat as springy's cork,
I clambered Lochnagar for the first time,
By Allt-na-Guibhsaich, startling a grouse.
My birthday, and my father's gift, the climb.

'Scotland's a pocket-hanky from the top. Dee's source and Don's
You'll see,' said he, all merriment, all cheer.
My sandals slithered, slipping on the shale.
The sun raised crops of freckles on his brow, and queer
And lovely clouds sailed silent by
My widening eye, mysterious as swans.

Suddenly, gaunt and gashed into the sky it soared
High as a bird, a grey bird rising far,
Wings bent against the wind in that massif
The darkling, stark motif of Lochnagar.

My father had not lied: like tents below,
Dwarfed tiny hills were pinned and fixed to heath
With Lochnagar, the general. They, his guards, beneath.

Three climbers died that day.
Fate flicked them off the crags like fragile wrens
Dropped from their lofty perch.
Happily tramping home, we passed the search
For that doomed trio. So, I learned the Gods
Are cruel to those mortals they don't love.
It ill behoves to anger those above.

At sixteen summers, gauche, with beau in tow
(Sunday, Hell's Angel. Weekdays, city clerk)
I scaled the Fox's Ladder. Halfway up
We stopped to drink cheap whisky from a cup.
I sang Lord Byron's song. Sank to the heather
And nuzzled naked moss like any lover.
My dull companion fretted, pining for
Bike, sandwiches, the football match he'd missed;
He liked to do his courting in the park
Clothes buttoned to the neck, where all was dark.
And, like a sheep that's never left the pen,
Found freedom frightening. He didn't come again.

A cargo train, at thirty I was back,
Laden with rucksacks, offspring trailing slow.
It was a vital matter they should know
This family member, icon, lover, shrine,
Boers' trek their Laocoon struggle past each pine
Tumbling and stumbling like loosened scree:
'We want a rest! A piece! A drink! A pee!'
Half-dragged, cajoled, unsteady candles guttering,
Their sire, a travelled mountaineer, muttering,
'I've climbed Mont Blanc. This mountain's just a pimple.
It's not the only bloody hill in Scotland.
You climb it every year, like some weird ritual.'

Forty. Marriage over. Kids half grown
I climbed the serpent, silver way alone,
And then it rained! Sweet waters bathed my face
The benison of that beloved place!
The winds that rained sharks' teeth across the tarn,
That shook the doors on cursing crofter's barn
Blew tatters of misogamy away,
Built arcs of rainbows, gleams across the grey.
Mountain of my delight, of all my knowings,
Your memory's a field of many sowings!

At fifty, with a Munro-bagging son,
I took Dod Byron's route by Invercauld.
'It's far. The heather's deep. You're none too *fit*,' he said
And like a faithful collie raced ahead,
Before. Then, sat and waited. Lit a fag,
A pencil line that smudged with every drag.
While up the tortoise slope, jaw set, face white,
Legs like cement, each steepening step a fight,
I toiled. He said, 'Quite soon the day will come
When this will be beyond you.' Dearest son,
When the time comes I cannot touch the skies
I'd like a bullet, straight between the eyes!

61

BENNACHIE

Charles Murray 1864–1941

There's Tap o' Noth, the Buck, Ben Newe,
Lonach, Ben Rinnes, Lochnagar,
Mount Keen, an' mony a Carn I trow
That's smored in mist ayont Braemar.
Bauld Ben Macdhui towers until
Ben Nevis looms, the laird o' a';
But Bennachie! Faith, yon's the hill
Rugs at the hairt when ye're awa!

Schiehallion, – ay, I've heard the name –
Ben More, the Ochils, Arthur's Seat,
Tak them an a' your hills o' fame
Wi' lochans leamin' at their feet;
But set me doon by Gadie side,
Or whaur the Glenton lies by Don –
The muircock an' the whaup for guide
Up Bennachie I'm rivin' on.

Syne on the Mither Tap sae far
Win'-cairdit clouds drift by abeen,
An' wast ower Keig stands Callievar
Wi' a' the warld to me, atween.
There's braver mountains ower the sea,
An' fairer haughs I've kent, but still
The Vale o' Alford! Bennachie!
Yon is the howe, an' this the hill!

Carn: Hill; *Rugs*: Tugs; *leamin'*: gleaming; *whaup*: curlew; *rivin'*: toiling;
Mither Tap: Mother Hilltop; *Win'-cairdit*: wind-carried; *wast*: west; *haughs*:
meadows; *howe*: vale

ON BEINN AN EOIN

Jenni Daiches b.1941

This is the oldest rock, this cauldron
of scalding winds, sandstone
churned by fire and flayed by ice.
Rock subtle with lichen, the seams
of peat stitched with tormentil and orchid.

The June sun has thrown a rainbow
over the shoulder of Beinn Eighe,
and Baosbheinn is fresh with snow.
I am too young to have business
here. My peat-hag prints are shallow.

It's my fiftieth year. My climb on the mountain's
bones maps the landscape's millions.
Its wisdom draws blood from my hands.
Its great age seethes in the wind.
Below darkness rolls in the river bed.

There is no battle. I am too young
to take on a mountain, to conquer the turreted
stone. I have not felt as deep
as the light that shivers the high head
of Liathach, though I say I have suffered.

I cross a bulwark swayed and smoothed
as if time is gentle. The rough path
consents. Inside the wind the rock
is held in silence and my boots ring.
I am welcome, although I am young.

63

BALLADE OF GOOD WHISKY
Norman MacCaig 1910–96

You whose ambition is to swim the Minch
Or write a drum concerto in B flat
Or run like Bannister or box like Lynch
Or find the Ark wrecked on Mount Ararat –
No special training's needed, thin or fat,
You'll do it if you never once supplant
As basis of your commissariat
Glenfiddich, Bruichladdich and Glengrant.

My own desires are small. In fact, I flinch
From heaving a heavenly Hindu from her ghat
Or hauling Loch Ness monsters, inch by inch,
Out of their wild and watery habitat.
I've no desire to be Jehoshaphat
Or toy with houris fetched from the Levant.
But give to me – *bis dat qui cito dat*[1] –
Glenfiddich, Braichladdich and Glengrant.

I would drink down, and think the feat a cinch,
The Congo, Volga, Amazon, La Platte,
And Tweed as chaser – a bargain, this, to clinch
In spite of *nota bene* and *caveat*
(Though what a feast must follow after that
Of Amplex, the divine deodorant!) –
If they ran – hear my heart go pit-a-pat! –
Glenfiddich, Bruichladdich and Glengrant.

[1]   he gives twice who gives promptly

Envoi

Chris! (whether perpendicular or flat
Or moving rather horribly aslant)
here is a toast that you won't scunner at –
Glenfiddich, Bruichladdich and Glengrant!

64

THE ANGELS' SHARE: A VIEW FROM BEN RINNES

Gordon Jarvie b.1941

An artist's sky like blue-stained glass
stretched the length and breadth of Strathspey,
so even before the tasting at Glenfarclas
this was a fine spring day.

Then after appraising the ten-year-old malt,
the fifteen, the twenty-one, the fabulous thirty ...
the snow-flecked patches on the higher hills
summoned me up to the sky's azure vault.

The Green Burn drains its snowmelt
plus a hint of peat off Ben Rinnes in the east,
begging to be mashed with barley and yeast
and magicked in oak casks by the hand of time.

The ben's bold peak stands out on a day like this
from afar in all directions: Ben Wyvis,
Mount Keen, Cairngorm, Lochnagar ...
I shall see all these hills from its pointed tor.

There's a zest and tang in the crystal air,
a thin haze of peat, pine and malt over Speyside
ascending to heaven. Is this the angels' share
rising on countless larks' wings, pride on pride?

They'd explained the angels' share: whisky lost over years
by seepage, evaporation and distillers' tears –
it's the difference between what is yielded up
by the uncasked barrel and what once went into it.

The haze over Speyside isn't any old haze:
it smokes from Glenlivet, Knockando, Tamdhu,
Chivas Regal, Tomintoul, Glenallachie, Cardhu,
Glenfiddich, Macallan, Aberlour, to mention a few.

Caperdonich, Ben Riach, Tormore and Longmorn,
Balvenie, Glen Moray and Mortlach: on and on.
This is a world-class distillation,
a roll-call to tempt any angel's discrimination.

I survey all of the above and more,
as I sit by the trig point of Ben Rinnes
inhaling an almost celestial panorama,
the air thick with larks and angels.

65

SING ME A SONG OF A LAD THAT IS GONE

Robert Louis Stevenson 1850–94

Sing me a song of a lad that is gone,
Say, could that lad be I?
Merry of soul he sailed on a day
Over the sea to Skye.

Mull was astern, Rum on the port,
Eigg on the starboard bow;
Glory of youth glowed in his soul:
Where is that glory now?

Sing me a song of a lad that is gone ...

Give me again all that was there,
Give me the sun that shone!
Give me the eyes, give me the soul,
Give me that lad that's gone!

Sing me a song of a lad that is gone ...

Billow and breeze, islands and seas,
Mountains of rain and sun,
All that was good, all that was fair,
All that was me is gone.

Sing me a song of a lad that is gone ...

66

WILL YE NO COME BACK AGAIN?

Lady Nairne 1766–1845

Bonnie Charlie's now awa,
Safely owre the friendly main;
Mony a heart will break in twa,
Should he ne'er come back again.

Chorus
> *Will ye no come back again?*
> *Will ye no come back again?*
> *Better loved ye canna be.*
> *Will ye no come back again?*

Ye trusted in your Hieland men,
They trusted you, dear Charlie;
They kent you hiding in the glen,
Your cleadin' was but barely.

English bribes were a' in vain,
An' e'en though puirer we may be;
Siller canna buy the heart
That beats aye for thine and thee.

We watched thee in the gloaming hour,
We watched thee in the morning grey;
Though thirty thousand pounds they'd gie,
Oh there's nane that would betray!

Sweet's the laverock's note and lang,
Lilting wildly up the glen;
But aye to me he sings ae sang,
Will ye no come back again?

cleadin': covering; *laverock*: skylark

ELGOL: TWO VIEWS

Meg Bateman b.1959

I looked at the old post-card,
the houses like a growth from the soil,
the peaks towering above them,
a sign of the majesty of God,
before an amenity was made of mountains,
or a divide between work and play,
between the sacred and the secular ...
And I passed the picture to the old man.

'Does it make you sad, Lachie?' I asked
as he scrutinised it in silence.
'Sad? Bah! Not at all!
I couldn't place her for a moment,'
and he pointed to a cow in the foreground.
'That's the Yellow Lady, the Red Lady's second calf –
I'd know any cow, you see,
that belonged here in my lifetime.'

MOUNTAIN BURN

Brenda G. Macrow b.1916

I am the mountain burn. I go
Where only hill-folk know;
Pitter-patter, splash and spatter,
Goblin laughter, elfin chatter!
I am a chain of silver under the moon;
A spell that breaks too soon;
Lost voices chuckling across the peat.
Or faery feet
Echoing where the dancing harebells blow.

The silent places know me. Trees,
Stately and cool,
Gaze at their green reflections where I flow
Into some shadowy pool.
I am a ribbon of light,
A flash of blinding-white
Foam where the pale sun lingers
Over the heathery waste.
And still my long green fingers
Probe with a surgeon's skill the perilous grey
Slopes of the ferny gorge to carve away
Granite and stone and bleached bone
To suit my changeling taste.
I am brilliant as the stars, and timeless;
Sad as the Earth, and strong
As mortal love. And through the long
Enchanted hours of sun and showers
I charm the hills with endless, rhymeless
Cadences of song.
And the dry reeds and rushes
Tremble and sigh, quiver and shake,
When the night wind hushes
With lullaby
The dreams that die, the hearts that break –
And only I am left awake ...

69

BALLAD OF THE MEN OF KNOYDART
Hamish Henderson 1919–2002

'Twas down by the farm of Scottas,
Lord Brocket walked one day,
And he saw a sight that worried him
Far more than he could say,
For the 'Seven Men of Knoydart'
Were doing what they'd planned –
They had staked their claims and were digging drains
On Brocket's Private Land.

'You bloody Reds,' Lord Brocket yelled,
'Wot's this you're doing 'ere?
It doesn't pay, as you'll find today,
To insult an English peer.
You're only Scottish half-wits
But I'll make you understand
You Highland swine, these hills are mine!
This is all Lord Brocket's land.

'I'll write to Arthur Woodburn, boys,
And they will let you know
That the Sacred Rights of Property
Will never be laid low.
With your stakes and tapes, I'll make you traipse
From Knoydart to the Rand.
You can dig for gold till you're stiff and cold –
But not on this 'ere land.'

Then up spoke the Men of Knoydart:
'Away and shut your trap,
For threats from a Saxon brewer's boy
We just won't give a rap.
O we are all ex-servicemen,
We fought against the Hun.
We can tell our enemies by now,
And Brocket, you are one!'

When he heard these words, that noble peer
Turned purple in the face.
He said, 'These Scottish savages
Are Britain's black disgrace.
It may be true that I've let some few
Thousand acres go to pot,
But I'd give each one to a London spiv
Before any goddam Scot!

'You're a crowd of Tartan Bolshies!
But I'll soon have you licked.
I'll write to the Court of Session
For an Interim Interdict.
I'll write to my London lawyers,
And they will understand.'
'Och, to hell with your London lawyers,
We want our Highland land.'

When Brocket heard these fighting words
He fell down in a swoon,
But they splashed his jowl with uisge
And he woke up mighty soon.
And he moaned, 'Those Dukes of Sutherland
Were right about the Scot.
If I had my way I'd start today
And clear the whole damn lot!'

Then up spoke the Men of Knoydart:
'You have no earthly right,
For this is the land of Scotland
And not the Isle of Wight.
When Scotland's proud Fianna[1]
With ten thousand lads is manned,
We'll show the world that Highlanders
Have a right to Scottish land.

'You may scream and yell, Lord Brocket –
You may rave and stamp and shout,
But the lamp we've lit in Knoydart
Will never now go out.
For Scotland's on the march, my boys –
We think it won't be long.
Roll on the day when the Knoydart Way
Is Scotland's battle song.'

[1] *Fianna*: band of warriors

THE LAND IS A' THE MARKISS'S
James MacTavish

From Kenmore
To Ben More
The land is a' the Markiss's.
The mossy knowes,
The heathery howes,
And ilka bonnie park is his.
The bearded goats,
The toozie stots,
And a' the braxy carcasses.
Ilk crofter's rent,
Ilk tinkler's tent
And ilka collie's bark is his.
The muir-cock's craw,
The piper's blaw,
The ghillie's hard day's wark is his.
From Kenmore
To Ben More
The warld is a' the Markiss's!

braxy: disease of sheep

THE LEGACY

Colin Will b.1942

We travelled north, father and son, to climb Suilven.
I thought my Forties memories
         might match his Nineties visions.
The Assynt hills, in just being, transcended both.
It still shocked me, when,
from the suddenly clearing mists,
an improbable verticality loomed behind Lochinver;
naked grey rock rising from soupy green hummocks.
The hills remain, eroded tusks of sandstone,
washed down from Greenland highlands
         before the ocean opened.
They lie like upturned ice-breakers,
as if Scotland planned to force the North-West Passage,
but held back, for aeons, upon a favourable augury.

Later, looking over Loch Maree to Slioch
I remember a pine marten stopping in the road.
It paused in the grassy mid-line
and stared at our Austen Seven
with our little post-war family.
My father drove on past traffic jams of sheep,
leaving a relict wonder
which has lasted over forty years.

Every father should leave his children mountains –
have Suilven, son. I still have mine.

THE ROAD AND THE MILES TO DUNDEE

Anon

Cauld winter was howlin o'er moor and o'er mountain
And wild was the surge of the dark rolling sea,
When I met about daybreak a bonnie young lassie
Wha asked me the road and the miles to Dundee.

Says I, 'My young lassie, I canna weel tell ye,
The road and the distance I canna weel gie.
But if ye'll permit me tae gang a wee bittie,
I'll show ye the road and the miles to Dundee.'

At once she consentit and gave me her airm,
Ne'er a word did I speir wha the lassie micht be,
She appeared like an angel in feature and form,
As she walked by my side on the road to Dundee.

At length wi the Howe o Strathmartine behind us,
The spires o the toun in full view we could see,
Said she, 'Gentle sir, I can never forget ye
For showing me far on the road to Dundee.'

I took the gowd pin from the scarf on my bosom
And said, 'Keep ye this in remembrance o me.'
Then bravely I kissed the sweet lips o the lassie,
E'er I parted wi her on the road to Dundee.

So here's to the lassie, I ne'er can forget her,
And ilka young laddie that's list'ning to me,
O never be sweer to convoy a young lassie
Though it's only to show her the road to Dundee.

sweer: reluctant

THE HILL ROAD TO ROBERTON
Will H. Ogilvie 1869–1963

The hill road to Roberton: Ale Water at our feet,
And grey hills and blue hills that melt away and meet,
With cotton flowers that wave to us and lone whaups that call,
And over all the Border mist – the soft mist over all.

When Scotland married England long, long ago,
The wind spun a wedding veil of moonlight and snow,
A veil of filmy silver that sun and rain had kissed,
And she left it to the Border in a soft grey mist.

And now the dreary distance doth wear it like a bride,
Out beyond the Langhope Burn and over Essenside,
By Borthwick Wa's and Redfordgreen and on to wild Buccleuch
And up the Ettrick Water till it fades into the blue.

The winding road to Roberton is little marked of wheels,
And lonely past Blawearie runs the track to Borthwickshiels,
Whitslade is slumbering undisturbed and down in Harden Glen
The tall trees murmur in their dreams of Wat's mosstrooping men.

A distant glint of silver, that is Ale's last goodbye,
Then Greatmoor and Windburgh against a purple sky,
The long line of the Carter, Teviotdale flung wide,
And a slight stir in the heather – a wind from the English side.

The hill road to Roberton's a steep road to climb,
But where your foot has crushed it you can smell the scented thyme,
And if your heart's a Border heart, look down to Harden Glen,
And hear the blue hills ringing with the restless hoofs again.

CHORAL SYMPHONY

Stewart Conn b.1936

The customary conversation
Gives way to applause
For the Orchestra. Then
A roar, as Karajan
Takes the stand. He raises
His baton: the strings sweep in.

During the interval, we remain
Seated. Two Edinburgh ladies
Behind us complain:
'Such Teutonic discipline
Breeds perfection,
Not Art.' Their companion agrees.

At the end they join in,
As the ovation goes on
And on. What has changed their tune?
We overhear: 'Weren't the Chorus
Superb!' 'As one voice.'
'And that lace, on Muriel's dress.'

A GUDE BUKE

Stephen Mulrine b.1937

Ah like a gude buke
a buke's aw ye need
jis settle doon
hiv a right gude read.

Ay, a gude buke's rerr
it makes ye think
nuthin tae beat it
bar a gude drink.

Ah like a gude buke
opens yer mine
a gude companion
tae pass the time.

See me wi a buke, bit
in a bus ur a train
canny whack it
wee wurld i yir ain.

Ay, ah like a gude buke
widny deny it
dje know thon wan
noo – whit dje cry it?

Awright, pal, skip it
awright, keep the heid
howm ah tae know
yir tryin tae read?

COD-LIVER OIL AND ORANGE JUICE
Carl MacDougall b.1941

It was oot o the east there came a big hard man,
Aw haw, aa the wey fae Brigton.

Chorus
Aw haw, Glory Hallelujah,
The cod-liver oil and the orange juice.

He went intae a pub and came oot paraletic,
Aw haw, the Buckie an the cider.

Does this bus go tae the Denny-Palais?
Aw haw, Ah'm lookin fur a lumber.

In the Denny-Palais he met Hairy Mary,
Aw haw, the floo'er o the Calton.

He says tae hur, Tell me hen are ye dancin?
Aw naw, it's jist the wey Ah'm staunin.

He says tae hur, Yer wan in a million.
Aw haw, so's yer chances.

Can Ah run ye hame Ah've goat a perr o trainers.
Aw haw, yer helluva funny.

Up the back close an doon the dunny
Aw naw, it wisnae fur the first time.

Her maw came oot tae go tae the didgy.
Aw haw, he buggert off sharpish.

She tried tae find the hard man, he's jined the Foreign Legion.
Aw haw, Sahara and the camels.

So Hairy Mary, she's had a wee baby.
Aw haw, it's faither's in the army.

dunny: basement; *didgy*: outside toilet

77

ALBA EINSTEIN
Robert Crawford b.1959

When proof of Einstein's Glaswegian birth
First hit the media everything else was dropped:
Logie Baird, Dundee painters, David Hume – all
Got the big E. Physics documentaries
Became peak viewing; Scots publishers hurled awa
MacDiarmid like an overbaked potato, and swooped
On the memorabilia: *Einstein Used My Fruitshop*,
Einstein in Old Postcards, Einstein's Bearsden Relatives.
Hot on their heels came the A. E. Fun Park,
Quantum Court, Glen Einstein Highland Malt.
Glasgow was booming. Scotland rose to its feet
At Albert Suppers where the Toast to the General Theory
Was given by footballers, panto-dames, or restaurateurs.
In the US an ageing lab technician recorded
How the Great Man when excited showed a telltale glottal stop.
He'd loved fiddlers' rallies. His favourite sport was curling.
Thanks to this, Scottish business expanded
Endlessly. His head grew toby-jug shaped,
Ideal for keyrings. He'd always worn brogues.
Ate bannocks in exile. As a wee boy he'd read *The Beano*.
His name brought new energy: our culture was solidly based
On pride in our hero, the Universal Scot.

STRANGER IN TOUN

Duncan Glen b.1933

You being frae Fife and born in Mallaig
I took you to see my Glasgow. The warm
humanity o Argyle Street and the distinctive
smell o the Subway. The haill lang length
o Sauchiehall Street and a quick visit
to the Mitchell Library and my first seat o learnin
at the table near the back. I took you for a walk
on Glasgow Green and into the People's Palace.
We stood by Clyde at the Broomielaw
and I spoke o steamers for Doon the Watter
and happy holidays at the Fair.
We went on tramride to the Art Gallery
and I stood wi you afore Rembrandt's
A Man in Armour. We had time
to haud haunds lookin oot to the country
frae the heichts o the University and stood
quait in the nave o the auld Cathedral. I showed
you Barlinnie Prison and the closes o daurkest Coocaddens
and the seikness o the Gorbals. We had a seat
in the sun in George Square wi its mony statues
and there was much Victoriana to be seen
afore high tea in famous Glasgow tea-room.
We had the best seats in Alhambra
Theatre for pantomime wi real Glasgow
comedians at the day's end.

Being frae Fife and born in Mallaig
you said,
'I liked the Rembrandt.'

HOME TOWN ELEGY:
FOR ABERDEEN IN SPRING

G. S. Fraser 1915–80

Glitter of mica at the windy corners,
Tar in the nostrils, under blue lamps budding
Like bubbles of glass and blue buds of a tree,
Night-shining shopfronts, or the sleek sun flooding
The broad abundant dying sprawl of the Dee:
For these and for their like my thoughts are mourners
That yet shall stand, though I come home no more,
Gasworks, white ballroom, and the red-brick baths
And salmon nets along a mile of shore,
Or beyond the municipal golf course, the moorland paths
And the country lying quiet and full of farms.
This is the shape of a land that outlasts a strategy
And is not to be taken with rhetoric or arms.
Or my own room, with a dozen books on the bed
(Too late, still musing what I mused, I lie
And read too lovingly what I have read),
Brantôme, Spinoza, Yeats, the bawdy and wise,
Continuing their interminable debate,
With no conclusion, they conclude too late,
When their wisdom has fallen like a grey pall on my eyes.
Syne we maun part, there sall be nane remeid –
Unless my country is my pride, indeed,

Or I can make my town that homely fame
That Byron has, from boys in Carden Place,
Struggling home with books to midday dinner,
For whom he is not the romantic sinner,
The careless writer, the tormented face,
The hectoring bully or the noble fool,
But just like Gordon or like Keith, a name:
A tall, proud statue at the Grammar School.

80

IN WINTER

John Purser b.1942

  driving through driving snow
the eye is mesmerised by the flow
of flakes, like migrants in a troubled time
travelling from distant wars. Rime
sticks to the wipers – to and fro
they sway and creak – a tired slow
defensive gesture of an old man's hand
passing through air, too tired to understand.
Clogged, burdened by memory, we know
no cure for our past useless shames;
endless irrelevance creeps in; we stow
facts into snowdrifts, all our claims
smothering. Wind, hard, level, cannot blow
even a gentle hollow in that deep white land:
the war has passed us over; there shall be no
blind prodding with a pole for names
buried beyond devotion.
                         Even so,
a dog, cold-nosed, still snuffles at the snow.

81

SNAW

J. M. Caie 1878–1949

Snaw,
Dingin' on slaw,
Quait, quait, far nae win's blaw,
Haps up bonnily the frost-grippit lan'.
Quait, quait, the bare trees stan',
Raisin' caul' fingers tae the deid, leiden lift,
Keppin' a' they can as the flakes doon drift.
Still, still,
The glen an' the hill,
Nae mair they echo the burnie's bit v'ice
That's tint, death-silent, awa neth the ice.
Soun'less, the warld is row'd up in sleep,
Dreamless an' deep,
Dreamless an' deep.
Niver a move but the saft doon-glidin'
O wee, wee fairies on fite steeds ridin',
Ridin', ridin', the haill earth hidin',
Till a' thing's awa'
An there's naething but snaw,
Snaw.

v'ice: voice; *fite*: white

82

THE GOWK

William Soutar 1898–1943

Half doun the hill where fa's the linn,
Far frae the flaught of folk,
I saw upon a lanely whin
A lanely singin gowk!
   Cuckoo, cuckoo;
And at my back
The howie hill stude up and spak,
   Cuckoo, cuckoo.

There was nae soun: the loupin linn
Hung frostit in its fa';
Nae bird was on the lanely whin
Sae white wi fleurs o snaw:
   Cuckoo, cuckoo;
I stude stane still
And saftly spak the howie hill:
   Cuckoo, cuckoo.

83

THE SMOKY SMIRR O RAIN

George Campbell Hay 1915–84

A misty mornin doon the shore wi a hushed an caller air,
an ne'er a breath frae East or Wast tie sway the rashes there,
a sweet, sweet scent frae Laggan's birks gaed breathin on its ain,
their branches hingin beaded in the smoky smirr o rain.

The hills aroond were silent wi the mist alang the braes.
The woods war derk an quaet wi dewy, glintin sprays.
The thrushes didna raise for me, as I gaed by alane,
but a wee, wee cheep at passin in the smoky smirr o rain.

Rock an stane lay glisterin on aa the heichs abune.
Cool an kind an whisperin it drifted gently doon,
till hill an howe war rowed in it, an land an sea were gane.
Aa was still an saft an silent in the smoky smirr o rain.

ON A ROMAN HELMET

Will H. Ogilvie 1869–1963

A helmet of the legion, this,
That long and deep hath lain,
Come back to taste the living kiss
Of sun and wind again.
Ah! touch it with a reverent hand,
For in its burnished dome
Lies here within this distant land
The glory that was Rome!

The tides of sixteen hundred years
Have flowed, and ebbed, and flowed,
And yet – I see the tossing spears
Come up the Roman Road;
While, high above the trumpets pealed,
The eagles lift and fall,
And all unseen, the War God's shield
Floats, guardian, over all.

Who marched beneath this gilded helm?
Who wore this casque a-shine?
A leader mighty in the realm?
A soldier of the line?
The proud patrician takes his rest
The spearman's bones beside,
And earth who knows their secret best
Gives this of all their pride!

With sunlight on this golden crest
Maybe some Roman guard,
Set free from duty, wandered west
Through memory's gates unbarred;
Or climbing Eildon cleft in three,
Grown sick at heart for home,
Looked eastward to the grey North Sea
That paved the road to Rome.

Or by the queen of Border streams
That flowed his camp beneath
Long dallied with the dearer dreams
Of love as old as death,
And doffed this helm to dry lips' need,
And dipped it in the tide,
And pledged in brimming wine of Tweed
Some maid on Tiber-side.

Years pass; and Time keeps tally,
And pride takes earth for tomb,
And down the Melrose valley
Corn grows and roses bloom;
The red suns set, the red suns rise,
The ploughs lift through the loam,
And in one earth-worn helmet lies
The majesty of Rome.

85

SONNET

R. D. Laing 1927–89

When I consider what you mean to me,
It is a fact I've come to realise
That you're my closest link to paradise
Despite what wise men try to make me see.

They caution us against idolatry
And tell us that we should not jeopardise
Immortal life for anything that dies:
And not to be bemused by mere beauty.

It seems ungracious not to take delight
In day because it turns so soon to night.
Eternity is always here to stay:
It's only you and I who fade away.

You are my here and now, my present tense.
I hope you will excuse my diffidence.

KINNAIRD HEAD

George Bruce 1909–2002

I go North, to cold, to home, to Kinnaird,
Fit monument for our time.

This is the outermost edge of Buchan.
Inland the seabirds range,
The tree's leaf has salt upon it,
The tree turns to the low stone wall.
And here a promontary rises towards Norway,
Irregular to the top of thin grey grass
Where the spindrift in storm lays its beads.
The water plugs in the cliff sides,
The gull cries from the clouds
This is the consummation of the plain.

O impregnable and very ancient rock,
Rejecting the violence of water,
Ignoring its accumulations and strategy,
You yield to history nothing.

87

LANDSCAPE WITH LAPWINGS

James Aitchison b.1938

It's another April, and a day
with all the seasons in it, with lapwings
falling out of sunlight into rain,
stalling on a squall and then tumbling
over the collapsing wall of air
to float in zones of weightlessness again.

And on a day like this in such a place –
a few square miles of moorland in a round
of rounded hills, rain clouds and scattered trees,
with water flowing clearly over stone –
in such a place I feel the weights slip off
the way a lapwing would if it were me.

The place might form a frame of reference
for calculating weightlessness, and all
the weathers that are in one April day,
for drawing what conclusions can be drawn
from lapwings tumbling in and out of light
with such a total lack of gravity.

JULY EVENING

Norman MacCaig 1910–96

A bird's voice chinks and tinkles
Alone in the gaunt reedbed –
Tiny silversmith
Working late in the evening.

I sit and listen. The rooftop
With a quill of smoke stuck in it
Wavers against the sky
In the dreamy heat of summer.

Flowers' closing time: bee lurches
Across the hayfield, singing
And feeling its drunken way
Round the air's invisible corners.

And grass is grace. And charlock
Is gold of its own bounty.
The broken chair by the wall
Is one with immortal landscapes.

Something has been completed
That everything is part of,
Something that will go on
Being completed forever.

89

YESTERDAY IN LAGGAN

Gordon Jarvie b.1941

It was such a day
of sunshine wall to wall,
of heat haze and the year's first frogs,
of blue hills stretching yonder.

It was such a day
of spring sun melting snow,
of fool's gold blazing off warm rocks,
of joy to be alive.

It was such a day
of hinted rainbows and dissolving light,
of fragile silences
flooding towards infinity

that I wished to be nowhere else,
doing nothing else,
in company of no one else,
and I wanted it to be forever.

BROODING REBUKED

Sydney Goodsir Smith 1915–75

Wha by takkin thocht
A cubit gains?
Or liftin airms aloft
Can stop the rains?

Wha by tricksickolatrie
Wins a new sel?
Or girnin at his weird
Flee's ain sel?

I ken o nane that did
Sanct or ye or me –
The lesson o the hevins reads
Juist be.

weird: fate; *Flee's*: Flies his

LIFE SUMMERTIME
Tessa Ransford b.1939

It is not yesterday that I would have
return, to pioneer again that path
I cut. Nor care I for the aftermath
Which hedges round the present life I live,
narrowing down the choices I must take
towards the future, and to my decline.
And yet without each effort now of mine
the world may be a future none can make.

I choose the sense of having loved to be
alive, and draw in fragrance from the past;
I balance amiably on present flowers
as each new moment sets another free;
and while the buzz of my intentions last
I build my honeycomb of future powers.

THE LINKS O' INNERLEVEN
William Graham 1800–86

Wha wad be free from doctors' bills –
From trash o' powders and o' pills –
Wad find a cure for a' his ills
    On the Links o' Innerleven.
For there whar lasses bleach their claes,
And bairnies toddle doun the braes,
The merry Golfer daily plays
    On the Links o' Innerleven.

Sae hie ye to the Golfers' ha',
And there, arranged alang the wa'
O' presses ye will see a raw
    At the Club o' Innerleven.
There from some friendly box ye'll draw
A club and second-handed ba' –
A Gourley pill's the best of a'
    For health at Innerleven.

And though the Golfer's sport be keen,
Yet oft upon the putting-green
He'll rest to gaze upon the scene
    That lies round Innerleven –
To trace the steamboat's crumpled way
Through Largo's loch-like silvery bay,
Or hear the hushing breakers play
    On the beach at Innerleven.

When in the evening of my days
I wish I could a cottage raise
Beneath the snugly sheltering braes
    O'erhanging Innerleven,
There in my plot before the door
I'd raise my vegetable store,
Or tug for supper at the oar
    In the bay near Innerleven.

But daily on thy matchless ground
I and my caddie would be found,
Describing still another round
    On thy Links, sweet Innerleven!
Would I care then for fortune's rubs
And a' their Kirk and State hubbubs,
While I could stump and swing my clubs
    On the Links o' Innerleven?

And when the evening grey sat doun,
I'd cast aside my tackit shoon,
And crack o' putter, cleek and spoon,
    Wi' a friend at Innerleven.
Syne o'er a glass o' Cameron Brig,
A nightcap we would doucely swig,
Laughing at Conservative and Whig,
    By the Links o' Innerleven.

Sung at the Autumn Meeting of the Innerleven Golfing Club, Fife, 1841

93

CANADIAN BOAT SONG
Anon

Chorus
   Fair these broad meads – these hoary woods are grand;
   But we are exiles from our fathers' land.

Listen to me, as when you heard our fathers
Sing long ago the song of other shores –
Listen to me, and then in chorus gather
All your deep voices, as ye pull your oars.

From the lone sheiling of the misty island
Mountains divide us, and the waste of seas –
Yet still the blood is strong, the heart is Highland,
And we in dreams behold the Hebrides.

We ne'er shall tread the fancy-haunted valley,
Where 'tween the dark hills creeps the small clear stream,
In arms around the patriarch banner rally,
Nor see the moon on royal tombstones gleam.

When the bold kindred, in the time long vanish'd,
Conquered the soil and fortified the keep –
No seer foretold the children would be banish'd
That a degenerate lord might boast his sheep.

Come foreign rage – let Discord burst in slaughter!
O then for clansmen true, and stern claymore –
The hearts that would have given their blood like water
Beat heavily beyond the Atlantic roar.

94

JOHN ANDERSON MY JO

Robert Burns 1759–96

John Anderson my jo, John,
When we were first acquent;
Your locks were like the raven,
Your bonny brow was brent;
But now your brow is beld, John,
Your locks are like the snow;
But blessings on your frosty pow,
John Anderson my jo.

John Anderson my jo, John,
We clamb the hill thegither;
And mony a canty day, John,
We've had wi' ane anither:
Now we maun totter doun, John,
And hand in hand we'll go,
And sleep thegither at the foot,
John Anderson my jo.

jo: mate, love; *brent*: (sun)burnt; *pow*: head; *clamb*: climbed; *canty*: happy

IN THE HIGHLANDS

Robert Louis Stevenson 1850–94

In the highlands, in the country places,
Where the old plain men have rosy faces,
And the young fair maidens
Quiet eyes;
Where essential silence cheers and blesses,
And forever in the hill-recesses
Her more lovely music
Broods and dies.

O to mount again where erst I haunted;
Where the old red hills are bird-enchanted,
And the low green meadows
Bright with sward;
And when even dies, the million-tinted,
And the night has come, and planets glinted,
Lo, the valley hollow
Lamp-bestarred!

O to dream, O to awake and wander
There, and with delight to take and render,
Through the trance of silence,
Quiet breath;
Lo! for there, among the flowers and grasses,
Only the mightier movement sounds and passes;
Only winds and rivers,
Life and death.

WILFUL WILL

Lesley Duncan

Black-bag me when I die.
Don't cry.
And no brass-handled coffins please.
Aesthetically I wince at these.

I used to dream of exiting with brio,
Accompanied by a Schubert Piano Trio
(The Second),
But now I've reckoned

That even that would be pretension
For one who craves no afterlife extension.
Let fire or worms then have their way.
Olé!

At the start of the new millennium, a Sunday newspaper ran a feature – somewhat macabre – entitled This Is Your Funeral, in which people contemplated their own funeral arrangements. This response could be interpreted as whistling in the wind of disbelief.

97

FOREWORD

Stuart Kermack

Sub specie aeternitatis your
death was less than nothing, sparrow-fall
on paltry planet, which had seen it all
a billion, billion, billion times before.
But my small universe burst at its core;
down a black hole was drawn beyond recall
so much that had, till then, been natural,
little seemed left that mattered any more.
My thoughts of you lack mental gravity,
weightless, in outer space they hurry-scurry,
blown by the cosmic wind of your decease.
Like tongues that probe a dental cavity,
they won't let be; but if, perhaps, I worry
them into fourteen lines, they'll rest in peace.

ANTE MORTEM

Syd Scroggie 1919–2006

I will attempt the Capel track
Old, stiff and retrograde
And get some pal to shove me on
Should resolution fade,
For I must see black Meikle Pap
Against a starry sky
And watch the dawn from Lochnagar
Once more before I die.

The golden plover whistled there
Before the Fall of Man
And you can hear the brittle croak
Of lonely ptarmigan,
No heather there but boulders bare
And quartz and granite grit
And ribs of snow, bleak, old and grey
As I remember it.

And if I do not make the top
Then sit me on a stone,
Some lichened rock among the screes
And leave me there alone.
Yes, leave me there alone to hear
Where spout and buttress are
And the breeze that stirs the little loch
On silent Lochnagar.

99

TWENTY-THIRD PSALM: SHEPHERD'S VERSION

Catherine Harvey

Wha is my Shepherd, weel I ken,
The Lord Himsel is He;
He leads me whaur the girse is green,
An burnies quaet that be.

Aft times I fain astray wad gang,
An wann'r far awa;
He fins me oot, He pits me richt,
An brings me hame an aw.

Tho I pass through the gruesome cleugh,
Fin I ken He is near;
His muckle crook will me defen,
Sae I hae nocht to fear.

Ilk comfort whilk a sheep could need,
His thouchtfu care provides;
The wolves an dogs may prowl aboot,
In safety me He hides.

His guidness an His mercy baith,
Nae doot will bide wi me,
While faulded on the fields o time
Or o eternity.

girse: grass; *cleugh*: ravine; *Fin*: Fine; *faulded*: folded

100

SONG

Robert Burns 1759–96

Contented wi' little, and cantie wi' mair,
Whene'er I forgather wi' Sorrow and Care,
I gie them a skelp, as they're creeping alang,
Wi' a cog o' gude swats and an auld Scottish sang.

I whiles claw the elbow o' troublesome thought;
But Man is a sodger, and Life is a faught:
My mirth and gude humour are coin in my pouch,
And my Freedom's my Lairdship nae monarch dare touch.

A towmond o' trouble, should that be my fa',
A night o' gude fellowship sowthers it a';
When at the blythe end o' our journey at last,
Wha the deil ever thinks o' the road he has past?

Blind Chance, let her snapper and stoyte on her way;
Be 't to me, be 't frae me, e'en let the jade gae:
Come Ease or come Travail; come Pleasure or Pain,
My warst word is – 'Welcome, and welcome again!'

cantie: cheerful; *swats*: beers; *towmond*: twelvemonth; *sowthers*: mends;
stoyte: lurch; *jade*: slut

NOTES

1   **EDWIN MORGAN** was born in Glasgow, and was Professor of English at Glasgow University until his retirement in 1980. From 1999 to 2002 he was Glasgow's first Laureate, and he became Scotland's first National Poet in 2004. This poem, Morgan's hymn to democracy, was commissioned for and read at the official opening of Scotland's new Parliament building in 2002: it is a manifesto for all Scotland's citizens, and is perhaps worth revisiting whenever we wonder where we're heading as a nation. (See also 19.)

2   **JAMES ROBERTSON** is a historian, novelist and poet. He wrote these two sonnets during a residency at the new Scottish Parliament in 2004. They are published in his *Voyage of Intent: Sonnets and Essays from the Scottish Parliament* (2005). Enric Miralles was the Spanish architect of the new building in Edinburgh, but sadly he died before his work's completion. (See 42 for more about James Robertson.)

3   **ROBERT LOUIS STEVENSON**'s poem 'Bright is the ring of words' was published in his *Songs of Travel* (1895), a year after his early death at 45. It has been set to music in the song-cycle by Ralph Vaughan Williams. Written from his exile in Samoa, the poem hints at the writer's nostalgia from his home in the tropics. (See also 65 and 95 for other 'Songs of Travel'.)

4   **ANDREW LANG** was a Selkirk-born Borderer and wrote this song from exile to his beloved home patch by the Tweed, for which he retained the deep affection of a London-based Scot. Ashestiel was the home of Walter Scott from 1804–11, when he was sheriff of Selkirk. Lang was a journalist, essayist and professional writer. He had a literary affinity with the coterie of poets who surrounded Swinburne and Rossetti, and many of his poems – like theirs – were modelled on old French rhyming

structures. For more about the ballade (spelt with an 'e'), see the note on the subject at 63 (for Norman MacCaig's 'Ballade of Good Whisky'). The Envoi of Lang's poem strikes an eco-friendly contemporary note, being a dig at the pollutant mills of Galashiels that even in the 1890s were threatening the Tweed's fishing.

5   **ROBERT CRAWFORD** is professor of Modern Scottish Literature at St Andrews University. This is an early poem, published in *The Scottish Assembly* (1990); like much of his work it offers an inventive, off-the-wall and forward-looking vision. Crawford's *Selected Poems* were published in 2005, and his *Scotland's Books: The Penguin History of Scottish Literature* in 2007. (See also 77.)

6   ANON, 'The Four Maries'. This poem is traditionally thought to have been written in *c.*1563 by Mary Hamilton, the 'me' of the poem's first stanza and one of the four Maries who acted as ladies-in-waiting to Mary Queen of Scots. The song is a traditional ballad and was listed in Francis J. Child's 5-volume *English and Scottish Popular Ballads* (1882–98).

7   **MAURICE LINDSAY** originally trained as a musician at the RSAMD. He says he particularly 'likes poetry which respects musical values', and that he 'always tries to deserve the title a reviewer in the *Times Literary Supplement* once bestowed on [him]: that of being an enjoyable poet'. With Lesley Duncan, he co-edited *The Edinburgh Book of Twentieth-Century Scottish Poetry* (2005).

8   ANON, 'The Bonny House o Airlie' is another historical ballad, this time describing an episode during the English Civil War between two hostile families – the Campbell earls of Argyll, supporting the English Parliamentarians, and the Ogilvie earls of Airlie, who supported King Charles I – and the destruction of the Ogilvie family's house at Airlie in 1640.

9   **THOMAS CAMPBELL** was a graduate of Glasgow University, and the author of popular Hanoverian war songs such as 'Ye Mariners of England', 'Hohenlinden' and 'The Battle of the Baltic'; he was also famous for his historical narrative poems such as 'Gertrude of Wyoming' and 'Lord Ullin's Daughter'.

10   **LIZ LOCHHEAD** trained at the Glasgow School of Art and began her career in the teaching profession. Today she is a well-loved performer, broadcaster, poet and playwright. She describes some of her poems as 'recitations', and the influence of the stage is evident in them when inimitably performed by her. Her poetry collections include *Dreaming Frankenstein* (1983) and *The Colours of Black and White* (2003). She was appointed Glasgow's second Laureate in 2005. (See also 51.)

11   **KIRKPATRICK DOBIE** was born in Dumfries in 1908 and lived nearly all of his long life there. He worked as a grain merchant in the family business, joining a literary group in the late 1960s when he started writing. His poetry developed out of this experience. In the best possible way much of it is local in focus, but it also confronted the big, universal themes with grace and toughness. His *Selected Poems* appeared in 1992.

12   **ELLIE MCDONALD** is a Dundonian, best known for her poetry in Scots in collections that include *The Gangan Fuit* (1991) and *Pathfinders* (2000). This family poem showcases her deftness as a poet in English.

13   **C. M. COSTIE** was an Orcadian, and spent most of her working life on the staff of Macrae and Robertson, solicitors, in Kirkwall. She wrote much Orkney dialect poetry and her *But End Ballads* were published locally under her pen-name 'Lex'. *Orkney Dialect Poems by C. M. Costie* appeared posthumously from the Kirkwall Press (1974), which also published her *Orkney Dialect Tales* (1976).

14   **RAYMOND VETTESE** was born in Arbroath, but has lived and worked in nearby Montrose for most of his life; so he now considers himself a 'Gable-endie'. He has worked as a journalist, librarian and teacher. Most of his poetry is in Scots, published in *The Richt Noise* (1988, winner of the Saltire Society's Best First Book award) and *A Keen New Air* (1995). He was president of the Scots Language Society from 1991 to 1994.

15   **DON PATERSON** was born and raised in Dundee and now lives at Kirriemuir, Angus. His four collections – *Nil Nil* (1993), *God's Gift to Women* (1997), *The Eyes* (1999) and *Landing Light* (2003) – have won a wide range of plaudits as well as the T. S. Eliot Award (twice), the Geoffrey Faber Memorial Award and the Whitbread Poetry Prize. He also works as a musician, writes plays, is poetry editor at Picador, and lectures part-time in creative writing at St Andrews University.

16   **GORDON JARVIE** lives in the East Neuk of Fife. He experienced this Glasgow epiphany in the summer of 2003, sitting munching at a lunch-time sandwich and watching the world go by. Fiftysomething years earlier he had played here with sisters and schoolmates. An old photograph from *The Bulletin* archive serendipitously re-appeared in *The Herald* later in 2003 to confirm the childhood recollections described in this poem, right down to the detail of the shiny tricycle. (See also 64 and 89.)

17   **ROBERT BURNS** is probably the only Scottish poet who requires no introduction here; his work stands as the keystone of Scottish poetry. This song is one of his best known love lyrics, as fresh today as when written in the 1790s. The source was said to be a popular street ballad written by a Lieutenant Hinches to his sweetheart shortly before going off to the wars. (See also 20, 56, 94 and 100.)

18   **EDWIN MUIR** wrote this love poem to his wife Willa Anderson, a Shetlander. They married in 1919 when they were working

in London, he as a literary journalist and she as a translator, novelist and teacher trainer. Together they translated the work of Kafka and a number of German writers. Muir's *Collected Poems* appeared in 1960 and a *Selected Poems* (1965) was edited by T. S. Eliot. Muir was born and brought up in Orkney. In 1950 he became Warden of Newbattle Abbey College, a residential adult education campus near Edinburgh; here he influenced writers such as George Mackay Brown and Tom Scott who were students.

19 **EDWIN MORGAN**'s poetry covers a very wide range, as revealed in the *Collected Poems* (1997) and *Collected Translations* (1996). This is one of his earlier love poems, a wistful expression of the power of memory and the transience of love. (See also 1.)

20 **ROBERT BURNS** was only twenty-three when he wrote this lyric, now one of the favourites. 'Of all the productions of Burns,' says Hazlitt, 'his pathetic and serious lovesongs, in the manner of the old ballads, are perhaps those which take the deepest and most lasting hold of the mind. Such are the lines to Mary Morison.'

21 **CHARLES JEFFERYS** was the popular Victorian songwriter and Sydney Nelson (1800–62) the composer of this famous party piece. The singer John McCormack immortalised it. Mary of Argyll is thought to have died young and has been identified as Mary Campbell, Burns's 'Highland Mary'.

22 **LADY JOHN SCOTT** based this song on a version written by her sweetheart, itself based on a much earlier version written around 1700. It became a favourite with Scottish soldiers serving in the Crimean War (1854–6). This version of the text originally appeared as a broadside ballad in Glasgow in the 1850s.

23 **JOSEPH MACLEOD** was Oxford educated and trained as a lawyer. He was a BBC wartime broadcaster and used the pseudonym Adam Drinan after the war to write poetry, often (as here) on

Scottish themes and with Gaelic cadences. His poetry shows economy of words, and can express humour as well as deep feeling. (Drinan is the name of a hamlet in Skye, home of his ancestors.)

24 **GEORGE BRUCE** hailed from 'the Broch' (Fraserburgh) and studied at the University of Aberdeen, where fellow students included Eric Linklater and Robert Kemp. He taught English before joining the BBC as a radio producer. This poem was for his wife Elizabeth, who pre-deceased him in 1994. A *Collected Poems* appeared in 2001; aged over ninety, he called it *Today Tomorrow*. (See also 86.)

25 **HILTON BROWN** wrote a variety of popular recitation pieces in the 1920s. His 'Glen, a sheep dog' was a great favourite, and was printed originally in *Punch*. His *The Second Lustre: A Miscellany of Verse* appeared in 1923, and he was generously anthologised in *Oor Mither Tongue* (ed. Ninian MacWhannell, 1937).

26 **BILL KEYS'** poem 'A Dug a Dug' has been a popular, anthologised recitation piece for many years; it is particularly well received in schools. It was first published in *GUM*, the Glasgow University student magazine in 1971. The author was a teacher of English, and some of his other poems appear in *Chapman*, No 97 (2000).

27 **JIMMY COPELAND**'s legendary *Shoogly Table Book of Verse* (Bramma, 1983) is his most famous work of 'party-piece poetry'. Extensive use of the glottal stop in 'The Blue Doo' is helpfully indicated in the text by the poet's widespread use of apostrophes. According to a spoof author's note at the beginning of this collection, the author was 'the greatest living Scottish folk-poet now living up his close at Charing Cross, Glasgow, the hub of the known universe'. Moreover, his writing was about to be awarded the 'Mobile Piece Prize' ... Copeland was also a film, stage and TV actor.

28 **DUNCAN MACRAE** wrote this poem in collaboration with Hugh Frater. It became something of a fixture on the BBC Hogmanay show in the 1950s, and Duncan's sometimes glaikit, sometimes pathetic, always deadpan rendition of this comic gem was a much-anticipated annual event for many years. Duncan Macrae was an early Citizens Theatre actor, and featured in many films of Scottish content, including *Whisky Galore* and *Para Handy*.

29 **ANON**, 'Three Craws'. This was a traditional, west-of-Scotland street song, rather like 'Ye cannae shove yer granny aff a bus'. It featured prominently in the repertoire of comic renditions of Duncan Macrae (see 28).

30 **THOMAS CAMPBELL** wrote 'The Parrot', like 'Lord Ullin's Daughter' (9) and 'Glenara', after visiting Mull. As a student at Glasgow University, he spent several summer holidays working as a tutor in the West Highlands. He was elected Rector of Glasgow University 1826–9, in competition against Sir Walter Scott.

31 **JIMMY COPELAND** wrote this poem in the days when the River Kelvin was a much more seriously polluted stream than it is today. In those days, it also had the BBC on its banks at Queen Margaret Drive, and – in the words of the poem – 'you know what they pour out from there ...'

32 **J. K. ANNAND** hailed from Edinburgh, attended Broughton Secondary School and Edinburgh University, and taught in the city. His bairn-rhymes in Scots are marked by characteristic vigour, wit and humour. They were published by Macdonald of Loanhead in three collections: *Sing it Aince for Pleisure* (1965), *Twice for Joy* (1973) and *Thrice to Show Ye* (1979), illustrated by Dennis Carabine. Annand was a gifted translator from Latin and German, and served as the editor of *Lines Review* and

later of *Lallans*, the Scots-language magazine, in the 1970s. (See also 54.)

33   **NORMAN MACCAIG** may have been raised as an Edinburgh townie, and indeed spent most of his working life there. But he wrote many anecdotal, deft and often humorous poems about his love of the countryside, its lifestyles and its creatures. In this playful poem he is content to be the butt of the joke. (See also 63 and 88.)

34   **MATT MCGINN** was a Glaswegian folk musician, songwriter, singer and humorist. *McGinn of the Calton* (Glasgow District Libraries, 1987) was a collection of his best-known work, and *Fry the Little Fishes* (1975) is autobiographical. He had an international following, and some of his songs were performed by Pete Seeger and Tom Paxton. He was also highly political, with a degree in the subject from Oxford, and was a member of the Communist Party at a time when that frightened the authorities.

35   **MARION ANGUS** was born and raised in Arbroath, where her father was a minister. Her poetry is influenced by the traditional ballad repertoire. A *Selected Poems* (1950) was edited by Maurice Lindsay, and a more recent selection is contained in *Voices from their Ain Countrie* (ASLS, 2006), a volume she shares with Violet Jacob (see 41), her contemporary and neighbour.

36   **IAN MCFADYEN** teaches at Peebles High School and started writing poems for his own children when they were small. He took inspiration from the way young children are thrilled by seeing new things – in this case an owl. This poem started one autumn night with the arrival of some tawny owls in a sycamore tree near the writer's home. He took his children out to peer at the visitors; the owls peered back. The author writes here in the Scots his parents and grandparents spoke to him when he was a child.

37   **ANON**, 'Aiken Drum'. Like 'The Cooper o' Fife' (44), 'Three Craws' (29), 'Wee Willie Winkie' and many others, this was a popular bairn-sang. In Robert Chambers's 1826 version (in *The Popular Rhymes of Scotland*), the chorus line reads 'And he played upon a razor ...'

38   **WILMA HORSBRUGH** was born at Blanefield, Stirlingshire. In the 1930s she contributed poems for broadcasting by 'Aunt Kathleen' (Garscadden) on the pioneering BBC Scotland Children's Hour. She produced some of her 'building rhymes' and recitations to entertain young children who were long-stay TB patients in hospital at Bannockburn. Several of her most popular poems are in the form of rhyming stories that repeat themselves, with the verses getting longer and longer. Her collection *The Bold Bad Bus and Other Rhyming Stories* was published by the BBC in 1973.

39   **WILLIAM TOPAZ MCGONAGALL** was a Dundonian and started life as a handloom weaver. As a young man he had a keen interest in theatre, and became an amateur actor. The poems started coming in 1878, and *Poetic Gems* (1890) went into many reprints. His work owes something to the tradition of humorous folk recitation, not to mention the noble Victorian theatrical art of declamation.

40   **M. C. SMITH** is supposed to have been the Kirkcaldy mother of a child at boarding school in Edinburgh in the early part of the 20th century. 'The Boy in the Train' is a localised version of the 'Are we nearly there?' refrain that remains well known today to all parents of small children on even the shortest journeys. It was a popular party piece in the 1930s. The 'queer-like smell' signalling arrival at Kirkcaldy in those days came from the town's linoleum factories.

41   **VIOLET JACOB** was the poetess of Angus, her native county, and a member of the Kennedy-Erskine family from the House of Dun, near Montrose (now in the care of the National Trust

for Scotland). She used her guid Scots tongue in the company of her estate workers. After marriage, she lived in India for many years before returning to her native heath. She wrote fiction as well as poetry, and the latest selection of the latter is published in *Voices from their Ain Countrie* (ASLS, 2006), a volume she shares with Marion Angus (see 35).

42   **JAMES ROBERTSON** studied history at Edinburgh University and was appointed first holder of the Brownsbank Writing Fellowship in 1993, based at Hugh MacDiarmid's former home near Biggar. As well as writing poetry, Robertson runs the Kettillonia imprint and has written several novels, including *The Fanatic* (2000), *Joseph Knight* (2003) and *The Tale of Gideon Mack* (2006). *Joseph Knight* won the Saltire as well as the Scottish Arts Council Book of the Year Awards for 2003–4. With Matthew Fitt (see next entry) he collaborated to write *Blethertoun Braes: Manky Mingin Rhymes fae a Scottish Toun* (Itchy Coo, 2004), from which this and the next poem are taken.

43   **MATTHEW FITT** was born in Dundee, and is a poet and novelist who writes mainly in Scots. He has held various writing fellowships and has been the Itchy Coo imprint's Schools Officer since 2002. He has also been a tutor in creative writing in Scots for all age groups. His innovative novel in Scots *But n Ben A-Go-Go* (Luath, 2000) was well received.

44   **ANON**, 'The Cooper o' Fife'. Another popular bairn-sang. See also 29, 37 and 44 for others.

45   **DAVID C. PURDIE** dedicated this poem to George Philp (an indefatigable Scots bigger) after hearing the latter talk about how, as far as the Scots tongue is concerned, there are 'biggers' and 'buggers' – those who try to preserve and promote Scots and those who disparage and rubbish it. He then applied the two words to his own working background in the building trade.

46 **MARGARET GREEN** submitted this poem to the BBC radio programme *McGregor's Gathering*, hosted by folk singer Jimmie McGregor, in the 1980s. It appeared in a follow-up anthology *Poems from McGregor's Gathering* (BBC Publications, 1987), and was later anthologised in *The Kist* (1996). Margaret Green was living in Glasgow at the time.

47 **R. S. RICHARD** was a teacher, artist and poet in Ayrshire and later in Chicago. Some of his poetry appeared in *The Herald* in the 1970s. In the 1990s a memorial exhibition of his work was organised by former colleagues and students at the McKechnie Institute, Girvan.

48 **TOM LEONARD** was a member of Philip Hobsbaum's Glasgow writers' group in the 1960s, along with James Kelman, Alastair Gray, Liz Lochhead and others. His *Six Glasgow Poems* appeared in 1969, and it was evident from the start that much of his poetry would revolve around the politics of 'langwij'; in his case Glasgow demotic. His *Intimate Voices: Selected Work 1965–83* (1984) was banned from school libraries in Central Region in the same year that it shared the Scottish Book of the Year award. (See also 55.)

49 **WILLIAM HERSHAW** is a Fifer, a musician and a teacher of English. This poem shows the poet as teacher and (for his sins, perhaps?) examination marker. Hershaw's poetry is mainly in Scots, and is published in *The Cowdenbeath Man* (Scottish Cultural Press, 1997) and *Fifty Fife Sonnets: Coarse and Fine* (Akros, 2006). He also runs a pamphlet imprint called Touch the Earth; this issued his *Winter Song*, winner of the 2003 Callum Macdonald Memorial Award for best poetry pamphlet. (See also 52.)

50 **NANCY NICOLSON** is a teacher in Edinburgh. Herself a country bairn she went to school in Wick, where home and school appeared to her to resemble 'two different countries'. Based on Nancy's recollections, this song tells the story of home *v.*

school English in the experience of one child. Nowadays, of course, schools are encouraged to value the language bairns bring to school a little more positively.

51 **LIZ LOCHHEAD.** This is an example of a poem that has to be read aloud in order to draw attention to the differences between the two languages, everyday Scots and formal English. As well as being a poet, Liz Lochhead is also a playwright and she well knows how to read her work aloud to wonderful effect. (See also 10.)

52 **WILLIAM HERSHAW** bases this poem on the oft-times hard professional experience of a teacher. He is head of English at Beath High School, Cowdenbeath. The poem comes from his collection, *The Cowdenbeath Man* (1997). (See also 49.)

53 **JACKIE KAY** was born and brought up in Glasgow, a black child of white adoptive parents, and now lives in England. She has published four poetry collections, two short story collections and a novel. She teaches creative writing at Newcastle University.

54 **J. K. ANNAND** was an Edinburgh teacher, and is best remembered for his bairnsangs. (See also 32.) He served in the Royal Navy during World War 2.

55 **TOM LEONARD** was born and brought up in Pollok in Glasgow, and now lives in the city's West End. Politically radical, Leonard satirises the Establishment, big business, denominational religion and their attendant hypocrisies. *Unrelated Incidents* powerfully demonstrate Tom Leonard's ear for the nuances of various demotic ideolects. (See also 48.)

56 **ROBERT BURNS.** This poem, like 'To a Mouse', was composed by Burns at the plough, when he farmed at Mossgiel, near Mauchline, with his brother. Both poems came to him in the course of his ploughing, and he wrote them out at the farmhouse in the evening.

57   **DOUGLAS J. FRASER** was a keen photographer, painter and hill-walker as well as a poet. He published poetry in the Scottish Mountaineering Club's *SMC Journal*, and his collections *Landscape of Delight* (1967), *Rhymes o Auld Reekie* (1973) and *Where the Dark Branches Part* (1977) were published by Macdonald of Loanhead.

58   **ANON**, 'I shall leave tonight from Euston'. This poem is said to have been inscribed originally on the door of the Ryvoan Bothy in the northern Cairngorms (by a vandal?). It was fortunately copied down before the door was destroyed (burnt down, perhaps by another vandal). The text appeared in print in 1945 in the Fell and Rock Climbing Club's *FRCC Journal*, and has been subsequently anthologised. It was probably written in the 1930s.

59   **LORD BYRON** was raised in Aberdeen, where he attended the town's Grammar School. Summer holidays with relatives on Donside probably sowed the seed for his poem about Lochnagar. The poem refers to the fact that several of his maternal ancestors, the Gordons of Gight, fought on the Jacobite side at Culloden. Byron moved to London when he inherited his title, and was sent to Harrow School in 1801. Thence to Cambridge, the Grand Tour, residence in Italy, and finally the Greek War of Independence (from the Turks) and death at Missolonghi probably from dysentery at the early age of 36. He never revisited Scotland, so 'Lochnagar' may be viewed as a sort of 'Home thoughts from abroad'.

60   **SHEENA BLACKHALL** has published numerous poetry collections, as well as being a fine storyteller and singer. She was brought up on Deeside, in Aberdeenshire, where her family have deep roots, and the North East is the main focus of her writing. Lochnagar is – of course – her favourite hill as well as being a frequent rendezvous.

61 **CHARLES MURRAY** was born at Alford, Aberdeenshire. He emigrated to South Africa in 1888, only returning to Scotland on his retirement in 1924. He served in the Boer War and later in the South African government, becoming its Secretary of Public Works in 1912. He started writing about Scotland from South Africa, and some of his nostalgia for his native area is evident in this poem. Many of his poems were energetic and tuneful, evocative of the Buchan countryside. Like Sheena Blackhall (60), he too had a favourite hill; and like Lord Byron's 'Lochnagar' (59), 'Bennachie' was one of Charles Murray's 'Home thoughts from abroad'.

62 **JENNI DAICHES** has written on various aspects of history and literature, including books on Robert Louis Stevenson and Naomi Mitchison, and histories of the Scots in Canada and the USA (where she was born). For many years she worked on publications at the National Museums of Scotland. This poem comes from her collection *Mediterranean* (1995); a more recent collection is *Smoke: A Poem Cycle* (2004).

63 **NORMAN MACCAIG** studied Classics at Edinburgh University before becoming a teacher. Latterly, he lectured in poetry at the University of Stirling. Although this was quite an early poem of MacCaig's (written before 1965), it wasn't published till the *Collected Poems* of 1990. Strictly speaking, a ballade (with an 'e' at the end) was a lyric poem comprising three stanzas of seven or – later – eight lines, rhyming *ababbcbc*, and each ending with the same eighth line for refrain. It usually finished with an envoi addressed to a prince or a patron, rhyming *cbbc*. One French poet who pioneered this intricate form was Francois Villon, and an early example in English was Chaucer's 'Complaynt of Venus'. MacCaig had obviously studied the form carefully. Christie MacLeod, addressee of this poem's envoi, was one of Norman's Assynt friends. (See also 33 and 88.)

64 **GORDON JARVIE** was inspired to write this poem at the end of a weekend visit in perfect spring weather to the Spirit of Speyside Whisky Festival in 2006. His hill poems are collected in *Climber's Calendar* (2007), and this was an occasion when his affinity for exploring the hills was not to be denied. (See also 16 and 89.)

65 **ROBERT LOUIS STEVENSON** wrote this version of 'The Skye Boat Song', according to his wife, as 'a set of verses more in harmony with the plaintive tune' than the hugely popular 'Jacobite' version by Sir Harold Boulton (a prolific English collector and author of songs and lyrics, including the rousing 'Glorious Devon'). Boulton's version was collected in 1879 by his collaborator Miss Annie MacLeod on a trip to Skye, and first published in *Songs of the North*, by Boulton and MacLeod, in 1884 (a decade before RLS's). The publication had a phenomenal success and went into numerous reprints, from which Miss MacLeod's name was latterly removed.

66 **LADY NAIRNE** (Carolina Oliphant) was a writer of ballads and songs, including 'The Hundred Pipers', 'The Land of the Leal' and 'The Rowan Tree'. She supported the Jacobite cause as well as the work of James Johnson's multi-volume collection *The Scots Musical Museum* (1787–1803, in which Robert Burns was also heavily involved).

67 **MEG BATEMAN** was born and grew up in Edinburgh. She writes poetry in English and Gaelic, a language she learned in adult life. She teaches at Sabhal Mòr Ostaig, the Gaelic college on Skye. Her collections include *Lightness and Other Poems* (1997) and her writing also features in *Eight Gaelic Poets* (ed. C Whyte, 1992).

68 **BRENDA G. MACROW** was well known as a Scottish outdoor or travel writer after World War Two. Her books included *Hills and Glens of Scotland* (1949) and *Kintail Scrapbook* (1948).

Her poetry appeared in the *Scots Magazine* and in collections *Unto the Hills* (1946) and *Hills and Glens* (1949), published by Oliver & Boyd. Her husband Adam was a photographer and helped illustrate some of her writing.

69 **HAMISH HENDERSON**. The vexed issue of land ownership in Knoydart here centres on the 1948 abortive but well publicised land raid by a group calling themselves the Seven Men of Knoydart. Lord Brocket, then owner, took them all to court and had them dispossessed of their land. Arthur Woodburn was a Labour MP and secretary of state for Scotland. Today much of the area is in the ownership of the John Muir Trust and some crofting is practised.

70 **JAMES MACTAVISH**. Property ownership gets a milder send-up here than in 69; this poem first appeared in *Punch* and was anthologised in *Oor Mither Tongue: An Anthology of Scots Vernacular Verse* (ed. Ninian MacWhannell, 1937). The 'Markiss' owned not just the world from Kenmore to Ben More in mid-Perthshire, and all the goats and cattle ('toozie stots') grazing there, but even all their 'braxy carcasses' (disease-ridden corpses). The 'Markiss' referred to was probably the Marquis of Breadalbane, whose seat was at Taymouth Castle, visited by Queen Victoria in 1842. They were a junior branch of the Campbells of Argyll. A more contemporary, succinct and sharper jest on the subject of land ownership was Alan Jackson's two-liner in *Scottish Poetry 3* (1968), entitled 'Young Politician':

'What a lovely, lovely moon.
And it's in the constituency too.'

71 **COLIN WILL** was librarian at the Royal Botanic Garden, in Edinburgh, and previously held the same position at the British Geological Survey. His poetry collections include *Thirteen Ways of Looking at the Highlands* (1996), from which this poem is taken, and *Sushi and Chips* (2006). He is a director of the StAnza Poetry Festival and lives in East Lothian.

72   **ANON**, 'The Road and the Miles to Dundee'. This was one of a large repertoire of walking songs (such as 'The Road to the Isles', 'The Uist Tramping Song' and 'By Yon Bonny Banks') written to help travellers and drovers while away the hours of getting from A to B before the days of public transport.

73   **WILL H. OGILVIE** was born near Kelso, where his parents farmed. After twelve years ranching in Australia as a young man, Ogilvie taught in the USA before returning to Britain and working as a journalist and civil servant. He retired to Ashkirk, Selkirkshire, in 1917, whence the hill road to Roberton snaked across the Border moors. This is one of his best-loved Border poems; and in 1993, thirty years after his death, a memorial cairn to Ogilvie was erected here. (See also 84.)

74   **STEWART CONN** grew up in Ayrshire, and later worked for many years for BBC Scotland as head of radio drama. He was Edinburgh's first official poet laureate from 2002 to 2005, and his poetry collections include *Stolen Light: Selected Poems* (1999) and *Ghosts at Cockcrow* (2005). He edited the popular anthology called *100 Favourite Scottish Poems* (2006).

75   **STEPHEN MULRINE** is perhaps best known – especially in schools – for his much anthologised poem 'The Coming of the Wee Malkies', which appeared in his pamphlet *Poems* (Akros, 1971). He is also a playwright, translator (from Russian), and has written for radio and television (including *Scotch and Wry*). He was a senior lecturer at Glasgow School of Art, and also a teacher of creative writing at Glasgow University.

76   **CARL MACDOUGALL** is a writer and broadcaster, most recently of the BBC2 series *Writing Scotland* (2004) and *Scots: The Language of the People* (2006). This ballad dates from the early 1960s, and younger readers may need to know that cod-liver oil and orange juice were available free to the general populace of Britain during and after World War 2 to help ensure they had a healthy diet in times of difficulty. Brigton (Bridgeton), Denny

(Denniston) and the Calton are neighbourhoods in the east end of Glasgow.

77   **ROBERT CRAWFORD** was born in Bellshill and attended Glasgow and Oxford Universities. He is co-editor of *The New Penguin Book of Scottish Verse* (2000), has written six poetry collections, is a formidable literary critic, and teaches at St Andrews University. This poem nicely updates Hugh MacDiarmid's 'Glasgow 1960'. (See also 5.)

78   **DUNCAN GLEN** trained in book design and typography at Edinburgh College of Art. As a teacher, he inaugurated and delivered degree courses at Preston and at Nottingham Trent University. As founder and editor of the journals *Akros* (1965–83) and *Zed* 2 0 (1991–), he vies with the late Callum Macdonald as one of the great and industrious enablers of a very wide and eclectic range of 20th-century Scottish poets. His own poetry favours the use of Scots and can convey considerable humour and joy of life. His *Selected Poems* was shortlisted for the Saltire Scottish Book of the Year award (2006).

79   **G. S. FRASER**, as this poem indicates, was schooled at Aberdeen Grammar School (like Byron – see 59), in Carden Place. Later he attended St Andrews University and trained as a journalist with the *Press & Journal*. He was a lecturer in English at Leicester University from 1958 till his death in 1980. He was a substantial critic, reviewing regularly for the *New Statesman* and the *Times Literary Supplement*. He is on record as being 'very conscious of the poem as something to be read aloud, though not in an over-dramatic manner'. He co-edited *The Collected Poems of Keith Douglas* (1951, 1966), whom he knew (slightly) on war service in Cairo.

80   **JOHN PURSER** is a crofter and lives on Skye. He hailed originally from Glasgow, and may be better known to readers as a composer, musicologist and broadcaster. His *Scotland's Music*

(1992, second edition 2007) won the McVitie's Scottish Writer of the Year award, and he has published three poetry collections.

81   **J. M. CAIE** was born at Banchory-Devenick on lower Deeside, just outside Aberdeen. He was raised at Enzie, in Morayshire, where his father was the minister. His main interest was in farming and he worked for the Scottish Board of Agriculture. A selection of his poetry was printed in *Ten North-East Poets* (1985, ed. Leslie Wheeler); his poem 'The Puddock' was anthologised in *Oor Mither Tongue* (1937), *The Kist* (1996) and *100 Favourite Scottish Poems* (2006), and is well known in schools.

82   **WILLIAM SOUTAR** was born and grew up in Perth. He served in the Navy during the First World War, and was diagnosed with spondylitis, or ossification of the spine. From 1930 he was bedridden, but throughout his time as an invalid he continued to write poetry in Scots and English. He also kept a diary, later published as *Diaries of a Dying Man* (1954, ed. Alexander Scott), which expresses a brave and optimistic outlook. In contrast, many of his lyrics are tinged with melancholy. Hugh MacDiarmid edited the *Collected Poems* (1948). Like much of Soutar, the Scots of this poem yields its best impact when read aloud.

83   **GEORGE CAMPBELL HAY** was brought up in Argyll, a son of the manse. Gaelic was not his mother tongue, but his linguistic skills helped him to fluency in this and several other European languages; and according to Iain Crichton Smith it was as a Gaelic poet that Hay achieved his greatest mastery. He served in North Africa in the war of 1939–45, which deeply affected his later life and work. His *Collected Poems and Songs* (ed. Michael Byrne) were published in 2000.

84   **WILL H. OGILVIE** is sometimes called 'the Border Kipling', partly because in his early manhood as a stock-drover and horse-breaker in Australia, he was a notable poet of Empire.

As this poem shows, he also shared Rudyard Kipling's interest in the Romans. Around the time of the First World War, he returned to Scotland and lived to a ripe old age in the Scottish Borders where he'd been born. There is also something of John Betjeman's style in his strong and regular rhymes and cadences. (See also 73.)

85   **R. D. LAING** was a Glaswegian, far better known as one of the iconic figures of 20th-century psychiatry than for his poetry. His *The Divided Self* (1960) was a ground-breaking critique of conventional psychiatry, and its tendency to depersonalise the patient. *Reason and Violence* (written with D. G. Cooper, 1964) was an explication of the thought of Jean-Paul Sartre. This little poem comes from *Sonnets* (1976), his only published book of poems.

86   **GEORGE BRUCE** hailed from Fraserburgh, in the far north-east of Scotland, and Kinnaird Head is the promontary just outside the town facing north to Spitzbergen and the North Pole – an elemental place. Much of his boyhood was spent among the rocks and coves of this coast. Bruce's father ran a family herring-curing business founded at the beginning of the 19th century. This poem first appeared in *Selected Poems* (1947), and soon became a favourite. Of his early poetry he says it eschews 'unessentials which would blur the precise outline', and tries 'to epitomise something of the physical nature of the east coast, and something of the spirit of the people who live and work there.' (See also 24.)

87   **JAMES AITCHISON** has published five fine collections of poetry, and a critical study of Edwin Muir, as well as student guides to grammar and writing. Formerly, he taught media studies at Napier University.

88   **NORMAN MACCAIG**. Another of MacCaig's fine nature poems, written 'in the dreamy heat of summer' (in *A Round of Applause*,

1962). The succinctness, humour, gravity and beauty of the moment provide the writer with this epiphany. (See also 33 and 63.)

89   **GORDON JARVIE** wrote this poem after a fine day on the hill; it forms part of his extended *Climber's Calendar* sequence (Loose Scree, 2007), and tries to articulate the slightly overwhelming realisation that life can't get any better than this. (See also 16 and 64.)

90   **SYDNEY GOODSIR SMITH** was New Zealand-born, and educated at Edinburgh and Oxford universities. He spent the war years in the War Office and joined the British Council's Edinburgh office in 1945. He soon became an Edinburgh character, and   under the influence of MacDiarmid – identified strongly with the use of Scots, which he handled effectively over a wide range of poetic subjects. He also wrote fiction, drama and criticism, and was for some years Art Critic of *The Scotsman*.

91   **TESSA RANSFORD** is one of Scotland's doughty cultural activists: founder of the Scottish Poetry Library and the School of Poets, editor of *Lines Review* (1988–98), president of Scottish PEN (2003–6), and begetter of the annual Callum Macdonald Memorial Award for poetry pamphlets. Born in India, and having also worked on the sub-continent, her poetry works towards the sort of holistic and quietist outlook that is perhaps more common in that part of the world than in the West. This poem appeared in *While It Is Yet Day* (1977) and in *Natural Selection* (Akros, 2001).

92   **WILLIAM GRAHAM** was a teacher, edited the *EIS Journal* for many years, and in 1851 became fifth President of the EIS. This poem appeared in his *Lectures, Sketches, Etc.* in 1873. The Innerleven links are no more, having occupied the site of the present-day Methil Power Station. It was here reputedly that

Old Tom Morris first saw play with the new Gutta Percha golf-ball in 1848, and at the Spring meeting of the Innerleven Golfing Club in that year Graham performed the first rendition of his song 'In Praise of Gutta Percha'. The punning reference in 'The Links o' Innerleven' to the Gourley pill is to the old 'feathery' golfball; and the nightcap of 'the noted distillery of Cameron Brig' would in those days have been the local whisky. (Cameron Brig now manufactures vodka.)

93   ANON, 'Canadian Boat Song'. This beautiful 'oar' song of exile and longing for the homeland is of disputed authorship, and first appeared in *Blackwood's Magazine* (1829). It was supposedly sung in Gaelic by Scottish exiles in Canada.

94   ROBERT BURNS wrote this, one of the great songs about love in old age, in 1793 when he was only thirty-five, a year before his early death. (For other Burns poems, see 17, 20, 56 and 100.)

95   ROBERT LOUIS STEVENSON was probably recalling his summer of 1881 spent at Braemar when writing this late poem. Here he completed his first novel, *Treasure Island*, and was captivated by the graciousness of the villagers as well as the beauty of the surroundings. In those days, there were many Gaelic speakers in Upper Deeside. (See also 3 and 65.)

96   LESLEY DUNCAN is the poetry editor of *The Herald*, where she has supervised the popular and civilising 'Poem of the Day' feature for many years. She co-edited *The Wallace Muse* (2005, with Elspeth King) and *The Edinburgh Book of Twentieth-Century Scottish Poetry* (2005, with Maurice Lindsay). Her occasional poetry and sometimes topical reflections appear in *The Herald*.

97   **STUART KERMACK** wrote this sonnet at the start of a sequence in which he tried to achieve some closure following the tragic death of a son at twenty-five, from cancer. The resulting publication *Sonnets for My Son* (Pinkfoot Press, 2001) was short-listed for the Callum Macdonald Memorial Award for best poetry pamphlet of that year.

98   **SYD SCROGGIE** was a keen mountaineer as well as an author and poet. A Lovat Scout in World War 2, he lost a leg and his sight in an explosion only weeks before the war's end; he was twenty-five. But his resulting disabilities did not prevent Syd from walking to his work, at D. C. Thomson's in Dundee. Nor did they keep him off his beloved hills, where friends and family acted as guides. He described his blindness memorably, as 'a sort of adventure'; and described himself as a hill 'gangrel' (vagabond). In any language, he was a famous character. His hill poetry appeared in *Give Me the Hills* (1978) and in Hamish Brown's anthologies of the hills.

99   **CATHERINE HARVEY**'s version of this famous hymn is familiar to many rural schoolchildren, and contains echoes of the Scots version of P. Hately Waddell, published in 1871. It may be sung to a variety of arrangements, the most famous being the tune 'Crimond'.

100   **ROBERT BURNS** wrote this song in 1794, two years before his early death. There are early intimations of mortality here; and in a letter to his friend Thomson he writes 'I have some thoughts of suggesting to you to prefix a vignette of me to my song, "Contented wi' little and cantie wi' mair", in order that the portrait of my face *and the picture of my mind* may go down the stream of time together.' As they have done.

INDEX OF POETS

100 Favourite Scottish Football Poems

Edited by Alistair Findlay
ISBN 1 906307 03 2 PBK £7.99

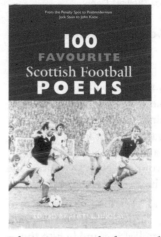

Poems to evoke the roar of the crowd. Poems to evoke the collective groans. Poems to capture the elation. Poems to capture the heartbreak. Poems by fans. Poems by critics. Poems about the highs and lows of Scottish football.

This collection captures the passion Scots feel about football, covering every aspect of the game, from World Cup heartbreak to one-on-ones with the goalie. Feel the thump of the tackle, the thrill of victory and the expectation of supporters. Become immersed in the emotion and personality of the game as these poems reflect human experience in its sheer diversity of feeling and being. The collection brings together popular culture with literature, fan with critic, and brings together subject matters as unlikely as the header and philosophy.

Ranging from the 1580 poem *The Bewteis of the Fute-ball* to poems by many of Scotland's best-known contemporary poets, including Hugh MacDiarmid, Norman MacCaig, Liz Lochhead and Edwin Morgan, the long and fascinating relationship between Scotland and football has never been encapsulated so well, nor has it meant so much.

This is a lively and entertaining selection with plenty to interest the football-sceptic reader... It's the social/cultural aspect that engages me the most. The range of experiences and emotions that the book touches on goes some way to explaining the depth and endurance of the game's appeal.
ANDREW PHILIP

100 Favourite Scottish Poems

Edited by Stewart Conn
ISBN 1 905222 61 0 PBK £7.99

100 Scottish Poems Large print

ISBN 1 905222 62 9 PBK £14.99

Poems to make you laugh. Poems to make you cry. Poems to make you think. Poems to savour. Poems to read out loud. To read again, and again. Scottish poems. Old favourites. New favourites. 100 of the best.

Scotland has a long history of producing outstanding poetry. From the humblest but-and-ben to the grandest castle, the nation has a great tradition of celebration and commemoration through poetry. 100 Favourite Scottish Poems – incorporating the top 20 best-loved poems as selected by a BBC Radio Scotland listener poll – ranges from ballads to Burns, from 'Proud Maisie' to 'The Queen of Sheba', and from 'Cuddle Doon' to 'The Jeelie Piece Song'.

Edited by Stewart Conn, poet and inaugural recipient of the Institute of Contemporary Scotland's Iain Crichton Smith Award for services to literature (2006).

Published in association with the Scottish Poetry Library, a unique national resource and advocate for the enriching art of poetry. Through its collections, publications, education and outreach work, the SPL aims to

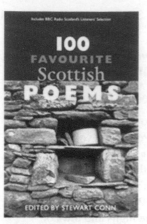

make the pleasures of poetry available as widely as possible.

Christmas Books, a nine-part series. Part I. The poet Stewart Conn has brought together 100 Favourite Scottish Poems, which is perfect for your Auntie Morag.
TIMES LITERARY SUPPLEMENT

Both wit and wisdom, and that fusion of the two which can touch the heart as well as the mind, distinguishes the work selected by Stewart Conn for his anthology 100 Favourite Scottish Poems (Luath Press and Scottish Poetry Library, £7.99). This lovely little book ranges from Dunbar to Douglas Dunn, taking in just about all the major and most of the minor Scottish poets of the centuries by means of their most memorable writing. THE SCOTSMAN

It is... a highly varied collection and one that should fulfill Conn's hopes of whetting the reader's appetite... this is both a taster and a volume of substance.
THE HERALD

The Souls of the Dead are Taking the Best Seats: 50 World Poets on War

Edited by Angus Calder/Beth Junor
ISBN 1 84282 032 X

Good war poetry breaks silence, restoring voice to those who have experienced horrors that lie beyond the language of everyday discourse.

From the clash of steel to the rumble of tanks, the sights and sounds of war have inspired poets of every nation since conflict was invented. In this timely new anthology, respected poet and historian Angus Calder and anti-war activist Beth Junor have drawn together a representation of war poetry from nations and cultures across the globe. Shared experience and powerful imagery combine to give this collection of poems an immediacy and poignancy that illustrate both the horror and the humanity that are distilled by the events that humankind calls war.

Ten Seasons

Edited by Gerry Loose
ISBN 1 905222 80 7 PBK £9.99

Ten Seasons grew out of Gerry Loose's three years as Poet in Residence at Glasgow's Botanic Gardens. This gathering of texts, along with stunning photographs, shows that poetry, although presented here on the page, in its most portable form, exists off the page, on scraps of material, in stone, even in water. The book both celebrates a particular residency and offers a rich resource for the interaction of botanic gardens and creative language. Plant-lovers and poetry-lovers will find much to enjoy in its pages.

Tweed Rivers: new writing and art inspired by rivers of the Tweed Catchment

Ken Cockburn & James Carter
ISBN 1 905222 25 4 PBK £9.99

There are many stories needing to be told about this 'Land of Tension', this frontier region, where ancient continents, historical political systems and armed hosts have clashed to bequeath a rich legacy that is recalled in song and etched into the very fabric of castles and towers. This project addresses this need through interpretation of key sites along the Tweed and its tributaries. Combining poetry, essays and short prose as well as a variety of visual media: from etchings and woodcuts through watercolours and acrylics to colour, black & white and pinhole photography. *Tweed Rivers* presents a contemporary reaction to this landscape, throwing over it – as Wordsworth would have had it – 'a certain colouring of the imagination'.

The Luath Burns Companion

John Cairney
ISBN 1 84282 000 1 PBK £10.00

Robert Burns was born in a thunderstorm and lived his brief life by flashes of lightning. So says John Cairney in his introduction. In those flashes his genius revealed itself.

This collection is not another 'complete works' but a personal selection from 'The Man Who Played Robert Burns'. This is very much John's book. His favourites are reproduced here and he talks about them with an obvious love of the man and his work. His depth of knowledge and understanding has been garnered over forty years of study, writing and performance.

The collection includes sixty poems, songs and other works; and an essay that explores Burns' life and influences, his triumphs and tragedies. This informed introduction provides the reader with an insight into Burns' world.

Burns' work has drama, passion, pathos and humour. His careful workmanship is concealed by the spontaneity of his verse. He was always a forward thinking man and remains a writer for the future.

Scots Poems to be read aloud

Collected by Stuart McHardy;
Intro by Tom Atkinson
ISBN 0 946487 81 2 PBK £5.00

 This personal
collection of well-
known and not-so-
well-known Scots
poems to read aloud
includes great works
of art and simple
pieces of questionable 'literary
merit'. With an emphasis on
humour it's a great companion
volume to Tom Atkinson's *Poems
to be Read Aloud: A Victorian
Drawing Room Entertainment* –
'much borrowed and rarely
returned...a book for reading
aloud in very good company,
preferably after a dram or twa'.

This is a book to encourage the
traditional Scottish ceilidh of song
and recitation. For those who love
poetry it's a wonderful anthology
to have to hand, and for all those
people who do not normally read
poetry, this collection is for you.

Poems to be read aloud

Intro by Tom Atkinson
ISBN 0 946487 00 6 PBK £5.00

Tom Atkinson's
personal selection
of doggerel and
verse ranging from
the tear-jerking
Green Eye of the
Yellow God to the
rarely-printed, bawdy *Eskimo Nell*.
Much borrowed and rarely
returned, this is a very popular
book. Great stuff for reading
aloud in good company, preferably
after a dram or twa.

Luath Press Limited

committed to publishing well written books worth reading

LUATH PRESS takes its name from Robert Burns, whose little collie Luath (*Gael.,* swift or nimble) tripped up Jean Armour at a wedding and gave him the chance to speak to the woman who was to be his wife and the abiding love of his life. Burns called one of 'The Twa Dogs' Luath after Cuchullin's hunting dog in Ossian's *Fingal*. Luath Press was established in 1981 in the heart of Burns country, and now resides a few steps up the road from Burns' first lodgings on Edinburgh's Royal Mile.

Luath offers you distinctive writing with a hint of unexpected pleasures.

Most bookshops in the UK, the US, Canada, Australia, New Zealand and parts of Europe either carry our books in stock or can order them for you. To order direct from us, please send a £sterling cheque, postal order, international money order or your credit card details (number, address of cardholder and expiry date) to us at the address below. Please add post and packing as follows: UK – £1.00 per delivery address; overseas surface mail – £2.50 per delivery address; overseas airmail – £3.50 for the first book to each delivery address, plus £1.00 for each additional book by airmail to the same address. If your order is a gift, we will happily enclose your card or message at no extra charge.

Luath Press Limited
543/2 Castlehill
The Royal Mile
Edinburgh EH1 2ND
Scotland

Telephone: 0131 225 4326 (24 hours)
Fax: 0131 225 4324
email: sales@luath.co.uk
Website: www.luath.co.uk

ILLUSTRATION: IAN KELLAS